WHAT PEOPLE ARE SAYING ABOUT
CREATING YOUR OWN ECONOMY

Dr. Dave Martin is one of the world's greatest communicators. He has the ability to share deep insights and profound knowledge all while making us laugh. His leadership principles will change the trajectory of your life and business if you put them into practice.

—John Maxwell
New York Times Best-Selling Author, Speaker, and World's #1 Leadership Expert

I don't know many people fuller of life and wisdom than Dr. Dave Martin. He is not only a tremendous speaker, but an awesome man of God who will nourish your soul.

—Larry Winters
Business Coach, Motivational Speaker, and Founder/ President of Leadership Team Development (LTD)

Dave Martin is a great leader. He is full of wisdom and practical tips that will help you become who God created you to be. I have known him for a long time, and he has made me better. If you're looking for a coach, look no further than Dr. Dave!

—Joel Osteen
Pastor at Lakewood Church and New York Times Best-Selling Author

Dr. Dave is one of the most gifted communicators I have ever encountered! A lot of people see how funny he is, and they recognize the richness of his voice, but under that is so much substance and insight!

—Steven Furtick
Best-Selling Author, GRAMMY® Award-winning songwriter and producer, and Lead Pastor of Elevation Church

You are impacting the lives of all those you coach and minister to, and I love your quote "The rest of your life will be the best of your life."

—Drew Brees
NFL Quarterback and Football Analyst

Dr. Dave Martin is one of the wisest men I know. You can describe him in three words: genius, genuine, and generous! Who would not want to follow a leader like that?

—Darius Daniels
Speaker, Coach, and Pastor of Change Church

Dave is one of America's greatest inspirational speakers and anointed success coaches. When you get around him, your life is going to another level.

—Jentezen Franklin
Pastor of Free Chapel Church and New York Times Best-Selling Author

Dr. Dave is a man on fire! I'm blessed to call him a friend. He has the information, the inspiration, and leads with incredible vision.

—Devon Franklin
New York Times Best-Selling Author, Award-Winning Producer, and International Speaker

Dave Martin brilliantly combines faith, strategy, and humor to propel you to success! His unique insights will inspire you and give you the steps to transform your dreams into reality!

—Terri Savelle Foy
Best-selling author, Television Host, and Your Cheerleader of Dreams

The common denominator in both championship athletes and successful individuals is a coach. Dave Martin is a coach who will teach you how to win in life.

—Grant Hill
NBA All-Star, Sports Executive, Basketball Analyst

Everyone gets knocked down. The key is getting back up. Dr. Dave will teach you how to get back up and go the distance in life.
—Evander Holyfield
Five-Time Heavyweight Champion of the World

WOW WOW WOW!!! Unequivocally, Dave Martin is one of the best speakers I've ever heard.
—Harvey MacKay
Businessman and New York Times Best-Selling Author

Dave Martin's teachings have transformed me, my family, and my business. He captures your attention and allows you to create a new "leadership crease" in your brain.
—Gillian Ortega
National Sales Director at Mary Kay Inc., Author and Coach

Dave Martin is an incredible leader, outstanding speaker, inspiring author, and impactful coach. His work impacts millions around the world. He understands viscerally what each of us needs to grow as he brings knowledge, vision, and spiritual understanding.
—Nido Qubein
President of High Point University,
Businessman, Philanthropist, and Author

Dr. Dave has a way of changing the way you look at things. And trust me, you will like what you see.
—Judah Smith
New York Times Best-Selling Author and Lead Pastor of Churchome

I've had a lot of great coaches in my day who made me great in baseball. Dr. Dave will make you great in life.
—Darryl Strawberry
Baseball All-Star, 3 Time World Series Champion, and Minister

CREATING YOUR OWN ECONOMY

Copyright © 2025 by Dr. Dave Martin

Published by AVAIL

All rights reserved. No portion of this book may be reproduced, stored in a retrieval system, or transmitted in any form or by any means—electronic, mechanical, photocopy, recording, scanning, or other—except for brief quotations in critical reviews or articles, without prior written permission of the author.

Scripture quotations marked KJV are taken from the King James Version of the Bible. Public domain. Scripture quotations marked NIV are taken from the Holy Bible, New International Version®, NIV®. Copyright © 1973, 1978, 1984, 2011 by Biblica, Inc.™ Used by permission of Zondervan. All rights reserved worldwide. www.zondervan.com. The "NIV" and "New International Version" are trademarks registered in the United States Patent and Trademark Office by Biblica, Inc.™ | Scripture quotations marked NKJV are taken from the New King James Version®. Copyright © 1982 by Thomas Nelson. Used by permission. All rights reserved. | Scripture quotations marked TLB are taken from The Living Bible copy- right © 1971 by Tyndale House Foundation. Used by permission of Tyndale House Publishers Inc., Carol Stream, Illinois 60188. All rights reserved. The Living Bible, TLB, and The Living Bible logo are registered trademarks of Tyndale House Publishers. | Scripture quotations marked NLT are taken from the Holy Bible, New Living Translation, copyright © 1996, 2004, 2015 by Tyndale House Foundation. Used by permission of Tyndale House Publishers, Inc., Carol Stream, Illinois 60188. All rights reserved. | Scripture quotations marked MSG are taken from THE MESSAGE, copyright © 1993, 1994, 1995, 1996, 2000, 2001, 2002 by Eugene H. Peterson. Used by permission of NavPress. All rights reserved. Represented by Tyndale House Publishers, Inc. | Scripture quotations marked GNT are from the Good News Translation in Today's English Version—Second Edition. Copyright © 1992 by American Bible Society. Used by Permission. Scripture quotations marked AMP taken from The Amplified Bible®, Copyright © 1960, 1962, 1963, 1968, 1971, 1972, 1973, 1975, 1977, 1995 by The Lockman Foundation. Used by permission. www.Lockman.org.

For foreign and subsidiary rights, contact the author.

Cover design by: Sara Young
Cover photo by: Kyla Stewart

ISBN: 978-1-964794-44-0   1 2 3 4 5 6 7 8 9 10

Printed in the United States of America

DR. DAVE MARTIN

CREATING YOUR OWN ECONOMY

A GUIDE TO FINANCIAL FREEDOM AND GENEROUS LIVING

CONTENTS

INTRODUCTION **WHY I WROTE THIS BOOK**..................13

CHAPTER 1. **EXTINGUISH YOUR LIMITING BELIEFS**.........17

CHAPTER 2. **UNDERSTAND GOD'S NATURE**................45

CHAPTER 3. **CREATE THE RIGHT MINDSET**.................61

CHAPTER 4. **EXAMINE YOUR HEART**......................91

CHAPTER 5. **SET YOUR PRIORITIES**...................... 109

CHAPTER 6. **PAY YOUR TITHE**............................133

CHAPTER 7. **DETERMINE TO DO THE WORK**.............. 149

CHAPTER 8. **GIVE AND PROSPER**........................ 165

CHAPTER 9. **ESTABLISH YOUR TRUE MOTIVES**............181

CONCLUSION **ON EARTH AS IT IS IN HEAVEN**............. 201

INTRODUCTION

WHY I WROTE THIS BOOK

BETWEEN TWO EXTREMES

In a world increasingly defined by economic uncertainty—marked by soaring inflation, rising interest rates, and a relentless cost of living—you may find yourself grappling with financial stress and insecurity. The daily news is often filled with tales of struggle, leaving countless individuals feeling trapped by circumstances beyond their control. Yet, amidst this chaos, there exists a transformative path: the power to create your own economy grounded in biblical principles.

I know this journey intimately. Growing up in a small town in Mississippi, with a poverty mentality, I was no stranger to the limitations and fears that accompany financial hardship. My early years were shaped by the belief that wealth was an elusive dream, reserved for the fortunate few. However, through faith, determination, and the timeless wisdom found in Scripture, I embarked on a journey that would lead me to not only break free from that mindset but also to embrace prosperity with a purpose.

This book is a testament to that journey. It is not merely a guide to financial success; it is a blueprint for living a life of abundance that aligns with your values and purpose. Drawing from biblical teachings and practical strategies, I will share the principles that transformed my life and can transform yours. You will learn how to cultivate a mindset of abundance, leverage your unique gifts, and navigate the complexities of today's economy with confidence and grace.

You see, God's principles of economics don't depend on what's happening in the world around us. They don't depend on the current mindset of Wall Street, they don't depend on the decisions the Federal Reserve makes, and they don't depend on the present spending levels of Congress or the economic platforms of our nation's two political parties. God's principles of economics work everywhere, all the time, for any person who will dare to believe them, embrace them, and implement them in his or her life, and they are never put on hold by the times in which we live or the economic turmoil we may experience.

Join me as we explore how to build a resilient personal economy that thrives regardless of external pressures. Together, we will challenge your prevailing narratives of scarcity, the limiting beliefs that have hindered you from having all that you were created to have and embrace a vision of prosperity that honors both your faith and your financial goals. It's time for you to break free from the constraints of the past and step into a future of prosperity and possibility. Your journey to creating your own economy begins now!

CHAPTER 1

EXTINGUISH YOUR LIMITING BELIEFS

Creating your own economy begins with what you believe. This book is based on the premise that you are a Bible believing Christian. So, we begin with gaining an understanding of what God's Word says about your finances, and how you can implement His financial principles into your everyday life. If you've been a Christian for any amount of time, there is no doubt that you have formed an opinion on what your finances should look like, based on your faith.

In fact, one of the main reasons I am writing this book is because God's financial principles have worked for me, and the interesting thing is that they started to work in my life during a time when the economy in our nation was just as bad as it is today. In 2009, when banks were failing and foreclosures were reaching record levels, Christine and I were in terrible financial straits. We were in heavy debt, we were upside-down on our mortgage, and we didn't have an income that could support a reasonable lifestyle or provide a foundation for our dreams. But it was during this time that I started discovering a lot of the eternal financial principles scattered throughout God's Word, and, when I dared to learn these principles, trust them, and implement them in my life, they started to work for me. I became debt-free for the first time in my life during one of the worst economic downturns in American history.

GOD'S INSTRUCTIONS

In 2009, good things started happening for me financially because I started to look in the right place for the solutions to my financial problems—in the pages of the Bible. In the same chapter where Paul had warned Timothy about the "perilous times" that were destined for humanity, he also gave Timothy the solution to all of mankind's problems when he said that "all Scripture is given by inspiration of God, and is profitable for doctrine, for reproof, for correction, for instruction in righteousness" (2 Timothy 3:16, KJV). In other words, the Bible contains answers to all of life's most vital questions, even financial questions and the questions that will arise during "perilous times." It offers "instruction in righteousness," the kind of instruction that is necessary for thriving in times of peril. So, the Bible has solutions for all of life's most difficult problems. God has not left us in the dark regarding anything that matters to us as human beings, and, if I believe this fact, then I can rest in the knowledge that God has already provided me with the answers I need for all the challenges I will face in life, including the challenge of achieving economic security. All I must do is find those answers, understand what they mean, believe them, and then put them to work in my life.

Of course, if the Bible does indeed contain all the right solutions for our day-to-day problems, then the best way to find those solutions and utilize them is to dig through the Word of God and then organize them into an internal reservoir of knowledge that can supply us with the wisdom we will need when we face particularly difficult circumstances. In fact, Joshua 1:8 tells us to "meditate on [the Word] day and night." The more you dig out the truths of God's Word and then meditate on those truths, the more spiritual insight you will have when you find yourself in a position where you need to draw upon it.

The entire message of the Bible can be summarized in this way: The Bible tells us how to get THERE (to heaven), and how to live while we're still HERE (on earth). The Bible has the wisdom and knowledge that we need to navigate any challenge that life thrusts upon us. What we need to do as Christians is to read and study and dig for that wisdom until we find it because it's always there, and then we need to believe it sincerely enough to act upon it.

Of course, one such problem that seems to confront just about every Christian at some point in his or her life is the same problem that plagued me for much of my life—the problem of finances. In fact, financial problems can be an ongoing challenge for a lot of believers. That's why believing people want to know how to prosper, and they want to know what God has to say about living the "abundant life" that He promised to us in John 10:10. Consequently, several years ago, I made a point of starting a lengthy study of every statement in the Bible regarding finances and every event in the Bible that involved finances. I wanted to start building a biblically based reservoir of information pertaining to financial security from God's point of view.

At the time I started this study, I was really struggling financially. As I explained earlier, I owned a house with an upside-down mortgage, I had way too much credit card debt, I had no long-term plans for retirement, I wasn't making enough money to sustain a reasonable lifestyle, and I had never even tried to create a family budget. So, I had a problem, but I wasn't the only one who had a problem at that time. It's important for you to understand that this all happened in the context of a catastrophic economic downturn that led to numerous bank failures, record levels of foreclosure (I ended up experiencing a foreclosure myself), and a degree of financial panic that the media referred to as the era of the "Great Recession." But God's wisdom is not conditional. His eternal truths don't change because of the shifting winds of politics or economics. His wisdom and inherent truths are steadfast and reliable, and they work all the time if we embrace them, believe them, and apply them with faith. It was during this season in my life that things started to turn around for me, simply because I found God's answers to my financial problems in the Bible, and I started putting those answers to work in my life despite the negative news that pervaded the airways and the despondent mood of the culture in which I was living.

Now, obviously, I wouldn't be writing this book if the outcome of my efforts had been unproductive. Instead, they were highly productive, and that is why I want to share the same principles that radically changed my life at a time when the idea of economic prosperity seemed like a mere fantasy. The good things that God did in my life at that time didn't transpire overnight, and there were some painful bumps along the way (and some unexpected miracles to help speed the process along). But the point I want to make is that God had the answers that I needed, and once I found those answers and started applying them to my life, things turned around for me in a very big way—despite the financial climate surrounding me. While many businesses were failing, my business started to prosper. While many people were going backward financially, Christine and I turned a corner and started moving forward. All around us, there was a recession, but in the Martin household, we were determined not to participate in that recession. Instead, we were determined to follow a more reliable path. And now, I want to share the eternal principles of that process with you. I want to expound on some of the principles of economics that I have found in the Bible, and I want to tell you how those principles can impact your life the same way they impacted mine.

Today, as in 2009, we are experiencing another serious economic downturn. Inflation, gas prices, interest rates, supply chain problems, and tax hikes, among other things, are working in tandem to push American families to the brink of financial ruin. But what I learned a decade and a half ago is that the growth of my finances, the growth of my business, the growth of my church, and the growth of my family don't depend on the ever-changing nature of the world's economy; they depend on the consistent application of biblical principles. In fact, many seemingly impossible obstacles have been overcome when people have made the decision to believe and apply the solid and time-tested truth of God's Word.

> **KNOW – BELIEVE – APPLY**

I want you to really take the time to understand this next section. God's laws will always overcome the world's obstacles. But, only to the degree of the following three principles.

1) The degree to which you KNOW the Word of God
2) The degree to which you BELIEVE the Word of God
3) The degree to which you APPLY the Word of God

So, what are the solid biblical principles that can put a person on the path to financial prosperity when all the people around him are fast approaching stagnation and fiscal ruin? It's impossible to believe and apply God's laws unless we first know His laws. I want to explain and illustrate God's truth and the laws that dictate those truths, so you can thoroughly understand them. But from that point on, it will be up to you to take advantage of these laws because, in the same way that it is impossible to believe and apply a divine principle that you do not know, it is also impossible to benefit from a divine principle that you DO know but are unwilling to obey with unwavering faith. These principles will work for the people who will work with them because the Word works for people who work the Word. But the Word of God won't work in your life or mine unless we are willing to work the Word once we have learned it and believed it.

At one point, Christine and I had $32,000 in debt and a combined income of about $500 per week. And, although inflation can make that amount of debt seem somewhat manageable, a little math will help you realize the true depths of our economic despair. We were in a bad place financially, and we knew it. Nevertheless, it was in the testing of the times in which we lived that we gained a more thorough understanding of the absolute reliability of God's financial laws. At a time when we were most desperate, we studied God's Word (the degree to which we KNOW the Word of God), we found the eternal principles that could turn our lives around (The degree to which we BELIEVE the Word of God), and we persistently applied those principles to our circumstances (The degree to which we APPLY the Word of God). See how that worked? And because we took that step of faith to study the Bible and implement its teachings, God blessed us and helped us in our journey toward financial health. But since Acts 10:34 tells us that "God is no respecter of persons" (KJV), God is also willing to do the same thing for you. If you learn His laws, believe His laws, and apply His laws, He is willing to change your life as well.

After all, if you can't believe God's promises pertaining to your finances, how can you believe His promises pertaining to anything else in your life?

How can you believe God when He tells you that one day He is going to raise your lifeless body from the grave and take you to heaven to live with Him forever?

How can you believe God when He tells you that He has forgiven you and accepted you without precondition?

How can you believe Him when He tells you that He "will remember [your] sins no more" (Hebrews 8:12)?

Sometimes, we Christians can be walking contradictions. We can believe God's promises for salvation, but not for healing. We can believe God's promises to help us during temptation, but we can't believe Him to help us through a financial challenge. What is it about us that causes us to pick and choose the promises we will believe and the promises we will reject? What is it about us that compels us to limit God's influence in certain areas of our lives while we openly proclaim His boundless abilities in other areas of our lives?

God wants to be a vital part of every aspect of your life. If there's an area of your life that is important to you, then that area of your life is important to God as well, and He wants to help you believe Him and glorify Him through that area of challenge and need. So, I beg you: don't put up a barrier before we even get started, a barrier of skepticism about the principles of economics that are scattered throughout God's Word. Give them a chance to impact you, change your thinking, and eventually change your life. Give me a chance to list them and explain how principles as old as the Bible itself can be relevant to your life today. Read this book with a willingness to believe and embrace these biblical financial principles—if they worked in my life, they'll work in yours. If you can believe some of what the Bible says, be willing to believe everything the Bible says, even if it "stretches" your concept of God and His willingness to be involved in your day-to-day life.

I think it's important for you to know that my understanding of God's Word and His financial promises to me weren't forged in a vacuum; they were forged in the throes of day-to-day living, and they were incrementally revealed to me. In fact, I started my financial education way over there on the opposite side of the pendulum. As I told you, I grew up in Mississippi in a poor household where poverty was equated with holiness. My father was the pastor of a tiny church, and he sincerely believed that prosperity was a symptom of sin. A neighbor with a nice car must have done something illegal or immoral if they were able to buy that car, and the fewer "worldly goods" we possessed, the more righteous we would be in God's eyes. Then later in life, I overcompensated for the extreme beliefs of my father and made my way to the other extreme side of the economic pendulum, where I spent most of my time around people who might be best described as "prosperity pastors." These were the men who owned diamond rings, Rolex watches, and private jets, and I viewed prosperity from their unique perspective for a little while.

But neither of these views seemed to be true in my life. I began searching God's Word for myself and I eventually experienced a complete transformation in my thinking. It was during this pivotal moment in my life that I met a man who became a good friend of mine, Wendell Smith, Pastor of City Church in Seattle, WA. Although Wendell died just six months after we met, he poured heavily into me during our short friendship and introduced me to a balanced perspective regarding biblical economics. He helped me see the errors in both approaches to prosperity and taught me that God's truth on economics lies somewhere between the two extremes.

One of the things this man taught me is that there is an important connection between prosperity and an individual's purpose. God certainly wants to bless all of us financially. We know that because the Bible is filled with people like Abraham, Jacob, Solomon, and Job, who were extremely wealthy according to the standards of their day. But this man helped me to understand that there was always a connection between God's purposes for these men and their earthly treasures. He helped me understand that God wants to bless us to help us fulfill the purposes He has established for our lives. If an individual is detached from the purpose that God has ordained for him, any blessings that God bestows upon that person will be wasted. Therefore, God's prosperity in my life is inextricably linked to my commitment to the purpose He has declared for my life. We are blessed to be a blessing! There is purpose in your prosperity!

So, with that in mind, you may want to ask yourself a couple of questions as we get started:

1) Does God really want me to be financially prosperous, or do I just want this prosperity for myself?
2) Since "the love of money is the root of all evil" (1 Timothy 6:10, KJV), can God trust me with a lot of money?

In other words, start determining right now the motivations that are driving you to seek more wealth and whether there is a connection between God's purpose for your life and the prosperity you desire.

I invite you to open your heart and open your mind as you prepare to open the pages of the chapters that lie ahead. I promise you that you will learn some things you have never learned before. You will also find a lot more biblical support for the truths you have already embraced, and I can assure you that this investment will make you more capable than you are right now of creating your own economy in an unpredictable and frightening world.

FAITH AND FINANCE

When it comes to faith and finances, we tend to migrate toward one of two extremes regarding God's principles of economic prosperity. One extreme is the view that I was force-fed as a child—the view that material possessions are sinful and that, like Mother Teresa, we must all embrace some sort of "vow of poverty" if we ever intend to be close to God. Growing up, we believed you had to be poor to go to heaven. We were so poor when we walked by the lake, the ducks would throw us food. We were so poor my dad told us that when the ice cream truck was playing music that meant they were out of ice cream. All jokes aside, we were so poor that the poor people in our church who received government assistance gave us their government cheese.

The other extreme is that God wants us to live in complete comfort and ease as we flaunt the material wealth He has bestowed upon us, so we can incite faith in others. We've all seen the results of this. Some people call this the prosperity gospel. But that is not the prosperity the Bible promises.

Actually, I no longer buy into either of these two extreme positions. There may be some elements of truth in each approach to the Bible's teachings, but, in my opinion, both views distort the intentions of Scripture and completely miss the heart of God. In the Bible, the people who flaunted their wealth were usually driven by pride and ended up paying a high price for their egotism. Hezekiah, for example, couldn't help himself. He was so proud of all the wealth that God had bestowed on him that he opened the storehouses of Judah and invited foreign dignitaries from Babylon to gaze at all his vast material resources (see 2 Chronicles 32:27-30). Then, just as the prophet Isaiah predicted would happen, the Babylonians invaded Judah to destroy the city of Jerusalem, ransack the temple and the treasuries, and carry the citizens of the country into captivity in Babylonia (see 2 Kings 20:16-18).

On the other hand, there is absolutely no connection anywhere in the Bible between wealth and sin. The list of prosperous people that God used over the course of about twenty-one centuries is quite lengthy. Abraham, Isaac, Jacob, Job, David, Solomon, Joseph of Arimathea, and Barnabas are just a few of the wealthy people God would use over the course of time to accomplish His purposes in the world. The connection between material wealth and sin takes place when one's love for wealth supersedes his love for God or supplants God's purposes for his life.

YOUR BELIEFS ABOUT MONEY WILL SHAPE YOUR FINANCIAL FUTURE

To move into the abundance God has for your life and to experience the fullness of what He has purposed for you, we must dispel some myths that you have heard. Many people would call these "limiting beliefs." Limiting beliefs will hinder you from receiving all God has for you. We must change our mindset and the way we think about money before we see our economic situation change.

TALK, THINK, AND LIVE LIKE IT

You are the offspring of a perfect God. Talk like it.

His covenant with you is forever. Think like it.

His prosperity is penetrating every area of your life. Live like it.

Prosperity is a thought-style before it becomes a life-style. Many of you may know the story I tell about how I got out of Mississippi a long time before I got Mississippi out of me. It's true; it was all a mindset. I left a small town, but the small-town mindset was still in me. So even though I moved geographically, I needed to change my mindset. I was "don't buy that" or "you don't need that." I believed the words I had grown up hearing.

"Money is not the key to happiness."

"Money is the root of all evil."

"Money won't make you happy."

I kind of felt like I just wanted to have enough money to know it couldn't buy me happiness. Have you ever felt like that? Have you heard some of those same phrases?

If those statements are true, then how do you explain the earliest verses of Genesis, before sin was even present in the world, God placed Adam in a lush garden that was renowned for its four great rivers, one of which marked a geographical area that was well known for its gold (see Genesis 2:11-12). So, at the very beginning of human history, before there was sin in the world, God placed Adam in a veritable gold mine, and God gave Adam all kinds of enjoyable and needful things like food, work, sleep, and sexual intimacy—things that were not sinful in and of themselves because sin was not yet a reality for human beings. But sin took hold when Adam and his descendants started to make all these "things" that God had given to them more important than God himself. Sin took hold when Adam and his offspring started to allow gold and food and work and sleep and sex and all the other great blessings of God to become the most important things in their lives while they consistently pushed God down to a lower position. You see, God designed man so that He could sit on the throne of man's heart while all of His external blessings were designed to enrich the man's life from the outside. But when man reversed this divine order—moving God to the outside of his life and moving "things" to the throne of his heart—that is when sin became the destructive force that it is today. And that explains why money is a blessing, but why the *love* of money is an affront to the Lord (see 1 Timothy 6:10).

LIMITING BELIEF #1: POVERTY IS A FORM OF GODLINESS

The idea that God wants his people to live in poverty is a gross misrepresentation of Scripture and a repudiation of God's original design in Genesis. Nevertheless, there are tens of millions of Christians in the world today who believe that poverty is godly and that poverty is good. For some reason, they equate poverty with humility (no such connection exists in the Bible), and they believe that living with a lack of life's necessities will somehow enable them to nurture a more perfect type of faith. They believe that people with money have somehow struck a deal with the devil and that the devil offers people money to coerce them to backslide.

There is nothing good about poverty. I don't see anything positive that can come out of poverty except maybe a greater appreciation for wealth. And I certainly don't see why God would allow the world's most evil people to possess all the wealth that He created for Adam while His most devoted servants suffer under a self-imposed death. I don't see why He would allow godless people who pay Him no mind to prosper while those who serve Him faithfully and obey His laws waste away in deficiency with no ability to raise themselves up. How is this supposed to glorify God? And what kind of message would this kind of biblical teaching send to those who have not yet surrendered their lives to Christ? "Come unto me all you who are weary and heavy laden, and I will make you even more poor and more heavy laden than you are right now." That's the kind of message some Christians adopt, but it's not the kind of message that's going to enable God to add "to the church daily those who [are] being saved" (Acts 2:47).

> **THE LORD WANTS THE BEST FOR HIS CHILDREN, BUT HIS BEST ALWAYS INVOLVES MORE THAN JUST MATERIAL SATISFACTION.**

LIMITING BELIEF #2: MATERIAL WEALTH DEFINES YOUR PROSPERITY

Some people will attempt to combine faith with selfishness and materialism, and this is the theological position that some modern preachers have condoned. The extreme voices that advocate the modern prosperity gospel tell us that God wants us to have all kinds of material riches . . . period! There are no preconditions for these blessings. There are no qualifications for them and never any mention of divine purpose. Instead, there's just a "blanket theology" for all believers that, if you want it, God wants you to have it. If you want it, all you must do is claim it for yourself because it's your birthright with absolutely no preconditions. But that's simply not true. We aren't blessed to be more selfish or to attain greater heights of self-reliance; we are blessed to be a blessing!

There are several biblical prerequisites for prosperity (which we will explore in depth), but the "extreme prosperity gospel," if honestly evaluated, is nothing more than a distortion of biblical truth that is motivated by the lust of the eyes, the lust of the flesh, and the pride of life (see 1 John 2:16). It is a particular theology that is heavy laden with the word "I" because it's all about what "I" want, what "I" desire, and what "I" think that "I" need. It is a distortion of God's laws designed to help us satisfy our selfish desires in a way that makes us feel righteous while we're feeding our sinful nature. But the Bible clearly teaches us that the "me first" approach to life is the wrong approach to life, so anything motivated by this kind of justification for material hoarding cannot be from God.

The Lord wants the best for His children, but His best always involves more than just material satisfaction. So somewhere between these two extremes, there's a place called "truth," and I want to help you discover that truth. I want to help you develop a mindset toward your finances that is biblically based, practically achievable, and theologically sound. I want to help you develop a theology around your personal economy and avoid the two extremes that ensnare so many people. I want to lead you to a healthy understanding of prosperity that can give rise to realistic goals and meaningful results in life.

Most of the objections that Christians tend to raise against the idea of prosperity are objections to the world's *system* for acquiring wealth—not to wealth itself. Wealth in and of itself is a good thing, a godly thing. As I have shown, before sin infected humans, God established Adam in a place that was full of health and wealth. So, God created wealth, God blessed Adam with wealth when Adam was perfect and sinless, and God has a "system" whereby His people can now tap into the wealth that He provided for them in the very beginning, when He created the world. This means that a balanced and appropriate approach to prosperity must not focus on the immorality of wealth because wealth in its essence is not immoral. Neither must it focus on the immortality of wealth because wealth in its essence is not immortal. Wealth is something in between moral and immoral, and it is something in between mortal and immortal. It is something good that God created for man's benefit to help man achieve the temporal, earthly purposes for which God created him, but it is simultaneously something that can awaken the vilest dispositions of a sinful heart. So, wealth is what we choose to make of it and what we choose to do with God's instructions regarding its proper use. Like a brick that can be used to build a schoolhouse or a house of ill repute, money has no moral nature; it's simply one of those "things" that God created for man's benefit that can simultaneously expose man's moral nature.

LIMITING BELIEF #3 MONEY IS EVIL

> **THE LOVE OF MONEY, NOT MONEY ITSELF, IS THE ROOT OF ALL EVIL.**

Money is not evil. It is the LOVE of money that is the root of all evil. This means, of course, that God doesn't want us to chase after wealth or take hold of it in ways that violate His moral laws. He doesn't want us to do sinful things to obtain it, and He doesn't want the wealth He has entrusted us to take His place on the throne of our hearts. He wants us to pursue wealth for the right reasons, acquire it in the right ways, and use it to do the right things. And if we will respect these divine boundaries, wealth is something that God will make available to us to help us achieve the destiny He has for our lives. He wants us to buy into His system of prosperity, not the world's system, so we can become who He wants us to be and achieve what He wants us to do in life. He wants us to buy into His system of prosperity, not the world's system because the world's approach to economics leads people farther away from Him and fills them with a gnawing sense of emptiness and meaninglessness. He wants us to live according to His "kingdom economy," not the world's economy, and, if we do, we will find that our prosperity is not only something He condones; it is a reliable way of living that is not subject to the ups and downs of global economics.

God does not want us dependent on the world's wealth. He wants us to have all He has created for us, to enjoy it, and to be conduits of His blessings to others.

I say it all the time: the purpose of our prosperity is like a water pipe. The purpose of a water pipe is not to get wet. The purpose of a water pipe is to distribute water, but in the process of distributing water, the pipes get wet. In your home, the water pipes carry water from room to room. The purpose of the pipe is not to get wet. It's just part of the process. God doesn't bless us so we can buy new stuff or get a bigger house. He doesn't mind you having that, but He blesses us so that we can be a blessing so that His blessings can flow through us. So, I pray every day, "Lord make me a distribution center of your blessing; bless me so that I can bless others." I will get blessed, but that's just part of the process. The true purpose is to be a blessing.

I haven't met a Christian yet who doesn't want to prosper under God's hand of blessing, but let's never forget the warning that the Bible puts forth regarding money: the *love* of money, not money itself, is the root of all evil. If money was so bad, why do we hug people when they give it to us? To love money—to place it above God in our hearts and lives—is to invite destruction upon our lives because an unrighteous attitude toward wealth can lead only to sorrow and vanity. As Paul explained to Timothy, it can cause us to be "pierced... through with many sorrows" (1 Timothy 6:10, KJV). But if we will allow God to enrich us in His way, according to the tenets of His eternal Word, we can enjoy a godly prosperity that is personally satisfying and financially resilient as we keep Him at the center of our lives. In other words, God's "system" for prosperity, if followed faithfully, will enable us to avoid sin and steer clear of the topsy-turvy, roller-coaster ride of worldly finance that is so often harmful to us spiritually because fear, greed, insecurity, or other unseemly motivations drive it.

By believing and implementing the biblical laws of prosperity, you will be able to prosper financially. Your life will begin to look different from those prospering through the world's system because you won't just prosper financially, but mentally, physically, emotionally, spiritually, and relationally. That's what the Godkind of prosperity can do for you.

The word translated *prosper* in the Bible is a word that goes far beyond the realm of finance. It's a word that speaks to a person's overall well-being because God wants us to prosper in every aspect of our lives. He wants us to be happy in our souls. He wants us to be healthy in our bodies, and He wants us to be positive about life and excited about the future, so we can represent Him well to the people we encounter along life's way. He wants us to be full of the peace, joy, and confidence that will attract unbelievers to Him, and that's precisely what His plan for prosperity is designed to do. Poverty can't do that. Poverty repels people, but a lifestyle of living under God's blessing and enjoying God's provision can make an impact on the people who are analyzing our lives.

THE BIBLE SAYS MORE ABOUT YOUR FINANCES THAN YOU THINK

In this chapter, I won't be listing the many promises of God regarding His willingness or ability to bless us, and I won't be describing any of the preconditions that God has set as prerequisites for His favorable involvement in our financial affairs. I will get to those important subjects later. At this early stage in our discussion, I just want to convey the idea that most Christians simply aren't aware of, and that is the volume of material in the Bible that addresses the subject of prosperity. A lot of Christians don't even know that our personal prosperity is a matter of great concern to the Lord and a matter of focused revelation in the Word of God.

> **GOD'S PROMISES OF PROSPERITY ARE ONLY HALF-BAKED INTO A LOT OF CHRISTIANS, EVEN THOSE WHO ARE AWARE OF THEM.**

Unfortunately, no believer can receive the benefits of a specific promise from God unless that believer is first aware that such a promise exists because if it's in the Bible, we must believe it before we can receive it. Furthermore, God's promises of prosperity are only half-baked into a lot of Christians, even those who are aware of them. Many have been taught extreme doctrines, have built a whole theology from an isolated scripture, or are unable to move Scripture from the mind and into the heart. The ignorance (lack of knowledge and understanding) existing in the body of Christ today when it comes to the subject of divine prosperity disheartens me. And the ignorance existing among church leaders and Bible teachers is even more disturbing because this area of theological "darkness," which pervades the contemporary church, is an area of biblical misinterpretation that is costing all of us in countless ways. It is costing us individually as we unnecessarily struggle through life, and it is costing us corporately as our churches and ministries are forced to suffer financial lack while the world perishes before our very eyes.

The fact of the matter is that God has already given us His best. He gave us His best when He gave us Jesus, so why would He deprive us now of all the good things He has made for us? Why would He deprive us now of all the good things He designed to help sustain us and propel us forward in life and ministry? Why, in the beginning, would He fill the world with such wealth for Adam and Eve but choose now to keep His people in poverty and want? Why would He fill the world with so many treasures and so many answers to mankind's needs (like medical remedies and natural resources) but leave it to the people who hate Him the most to discover those things, harness those things, and utilize those things to create wealth? The obvious answer is: He wouldn't.

Romans 8:32 says, "He who did not spare his own Son, but gave him up for us all—how will he not also, along with him, graciously give us all things?" That is the question that establishes the premise for this book. God's gift of His Son serves as an illustration of just how much He wants to bless us. It serves as an illustration of God's generous attitude toward the people He loves. God's goodness benefits Him as much or more as it benefits us because God has made us to reflect Himself. He has made us to be walking, talking advertisements for the Christian life. So just think about it: if God has designed you to be a living, breathing representative of His kingdom, why would He want you to live your entire life in poverty, scarcity, and lack? Why would He want you to live in misery, suffering, and constant need? That kind of lifestyle doesn't glorify Him in any way, and it certainly won't attract people to Him.

Obviously, there will be seasons in our lives when God will allow us to be tested or endure certain kinds of trials, including financial trials, and the Lord will allow these seasons of testing to nurture faith in our lives or achieve His purposes through our lives. But God wants us to live under the shadow of his blessing and to walk in His prosperity, and we need to know that about Him if we ever intend to rise above our current levels of achievement. If God intends to bless the world through us, we are going to need a lot more resources than we currently have at our disposal to impact a world of eight billion people in need. This really got into me back when my wife and I lived in a little government-assisted apartment. My mindset changed—I believed God really wanted me to do well in life. I HAD A PURPOSE, and I needed finances to fulfill that purpose.

Do you know why so many unbelievers prosper financially? They prosper because, whether they know it or not, they follow a lot of God's economic laws. Obviously, some unbelievers are bent on acquiring their wealth through illegal or unethical means. Some submit false insurance claims, cheat on their taxes, or sell stolen goods to unwary customers. But not all prosperous people are shady characters. They may not know the Lord or serve Him, but they still follow many of His principles. God's eternal principles of economics work when we implement them—whether we attribute them to God or not. These principles work for believers, too, because they are eternal principles designed to work for us if we work with them.

Unfortunately, many Christians just don't know the eternal principles of economics scattered throughout God's Word, and Christians can't activate the principles they do not know. In the chapters that follow, I want to expose you to the eternal principles of economics that have changed my life and the lives of countless others, past and present. I want to analyze the verses that present the financial laws explicitly taught in the biblical text and study the lives of the men who implemented them by faith to help you comprehend the long-term benefits of believing and applying those laws.

I realize that the subject of prosperity can be unsettling for many people because some of us have been around long enough to see the damage extreme teachings have done. I also know that current events can have a real impact on this subject as we face the realities of an economic climate that is both discouraging and frightening. And I understand the skepticism about another faith-based book that promises to use the Bible to teach them about financial affluence and a righteous way of attaining wealth.

> **SO, IF MONEY—HOW MUCH WE HAVE, HOW MUCH WE NEED, HOW WE MAKE IT, HOW WE USE IT—IS SO IMPORTANT TO GOD, THEN IT SHOULD BE IMPORTANT TO US TOO.**

But let's get real here: money plays an enormous role in our daily lives, and it's the main reason we get up and go to work each day. When we're not making money, we're spending money, trying to save money, or managing our money, so we can afford the things we need. Money is an important part of our lives, and money impacts just about every aspect of our lives. It also impacts virtually every aspect of church life and ministry. And that's why God wants to be personally involved in our finances. It's why He is so concerned about us having a proper relationship with our money. Something that consumes that much of our time and that much of our attention will demand His hands-on involvement because He wants us to have enough money to live without constant stress, and he wants us to have enough money to pursue the visions and dreams He has placed in our hearts for ourselves, our families, our businesses, and our churches.

In fact, God has told us candidly that "money is the answer for everything" (Ecclesiastes 10:19). God has told us without equivocation that, in this present world, money is the tool that can meet more of our needs and solve more of our problems than any other means we have at our disposal. So, if money—how much we have, how much we need, how we make it, and how we use it—is so important to God, then it should be important to us too. To think otherwise is to bury our heads in the sand and condemn ourselves to lives of limited achievement. And since the Bible has all the information, we will ever need to make wise decisions and live fulfilling lives, I believe we should look there, in the holy Scriptures, for the timeless wisdom we require when it comes to our finances. Besides, although money can't buy us happiness, neither can poverty. But money sure can solve a lot of our earthly problems.

You may have started reading this book because you need a miracle in your finances. Maybe you started reading it because you want to understand what the Bible says about prosperity. You may be reading this book because you want to fulfill your purpose and you're lacking the finances you need to fulfill that purpose. Your current situation may look impossible. The high inflation and extreme interest rates could seem insurmountable. Listen, today is not permanent. God can step into those areas of your life and turn the tide in your favor. In a moment, He can turn everything around.

If you've never explored the subject of money from a biblical perspective or if you've never been strongly motivated to learn about the Bible's promises and preconditions for prosperity, please don't remain ignorant about this vitally important subject. The Bible has a lot to say about money. Hundreds of biblical verses address this vital life concern, and Jesus had more to say about money during His earthly ministry than any other subject except the subject of love. Moreover, God knows that the devil preys upon our ignorance. God knows that Satan does his best work in the empty spaces of our uninformed minds, where there is no biblical knowledge to offset his lies, and the world sows its seeds of doubt and skepticism in those same empty spaces. So, let's fill those spaces with God's truth. Let's fill them with God's light. Let's fill them with a vast reservoir of God's promises concerning His desire to bless our finances and enrich our earthly lives, and let's fill them with an understanding of the Lord's requirements for living a life that is marked by His favor. Let's look directly into the Bible, so the straightforward promises of God's Word can clear away the cobwebs of erroneous thinking about wealth that may be clouding our minds, and let's use the rightly divided Word to set straight the confusion that theological extremism has caused.

If we, as Christians, can get our thinking right when it comes to the subject of money, we can get our believing right. And if we can get our believing right, we can get our behaviors right. And if we can get our behaviors right when it comes to our personal finances, we can plot the course for our own lives and determine their quality and outcome so that the rest of our lives will be the best of our lives.

CHAPTER 2

UNDERSTAND GOD'S NATURE

When we understand God's nature and His attitude toward money, things will start to change in our finances. As with anything in life, it all starts with understanding God and how He thinks. If we do this in all we do, we will begin to operate in the way we were created to function. Does God's nature come across in the Bible as selfish, or does God present Himself as one who bestows "more than enough" upon His people? Do we see a stingy God or a God of generosity? God freely gives! He loves to give; He loves to give so much that He gave His only Son! We can argue the meanings of certain passages of Scripture all day long, but in the end, the argument "for" or "against" prosperity comes down to a proper understanding of God Himself: who He is and what He is like. Simply put, God is a God of more abundance than our minds can possibly imagine, and He is a God who is compelled by His love to give. For these reasons, He is clearly revealed in Scripture as a God who bountifully blesses those who love Him and serve Him throughout their lives.

GOD'S NATURE DOES NOT HAVE TWO COMPETING SIDES

Quite often, when I teach about prosperity or when I describe God as a God of richness and abundance, I get reactions that remind me of the current political climate in our nation. In the United States right now, it seems like everybody has taken a "side." It seems like people are either positioned on the "left" or the "right" of every political argument. We are polarized. Few people are in the middle, and few are genuinely undecided. Unfortunately, it's pretty much the same in the Christian community when it comes to the subject of prosperity. People tend to lean toward one of the two extreme theological positions, and they tend to dig in their heels whenever they are challenged. Modern-day Christians tend to either elevate poverty as a spiritual benefit, or they tend to embrace the notion that God wants every Christian to have all the wealth he or she desires. However, both extremes stand in direct opposition to the revelation of God Himself.

Because I believe and teach that there is a promise of prosperity in the Bible that reflects God's abundant and giving nature, I am often referred to as a "health and wealth" preacher. But I'm not a "health and wealth" preacher. Of course, I'm not a "sickness and poverty" teacher either. I am a presenter of God and His truths, and I believe that God, by His very nature, wants His children to have enough to live and enough to give, but not enough to waste or to hoard—and that's what I believe the Bible means when it speaks of wealth and abundance.

I just don't understand why we feel the need to choose between excess and overindulgence on the one hand and scarcity and deficiency on the other when God's Word uses neither description to convey its image of our Creator or the abundant life He has promised to us?

I don't believe that God wants every believer to have a Lamborghini and a private jet, because every believer might not be able to handle that. Every believer might not do the right thing with their blessings. The Word of God tells us we must be good stewards of our money. I also don't believe that it's God's plan for me to work every day of my life and then come up short each month when the time rolls around to pay my mortgage. I don't believe it's God's plan for me to have to whip out a credit card every time I need a new pair of shoes for my son or some dental work for myself. I don't believe it's God's plan for me to be unable to give to my church or to help other people who have urgent needs. I don't believe it's God's plan for me to be stressed out all the time about money because something unexpected seems to happen to me every day that forces me to tap into my bank account and spend money I just don't have. And I can back these beliefs up with the Word of God.

How can a person provide for his or her family if that person is always running short of money? How can a person help advance the kingdom of God if he or she lacks the resources to do so? How can a person help a single mother pay her rent when he can't even pay his own rent? How can a person feel like they are contributing to the work of God when they are always on the receiving end, but never on the giving end of the generosity pipeline?

I'm not your typical prosperity gospel preacher, but I do believe God intends for us to be healthy and wealthy. He certainly doesn't want us to be sick and poor. I don't believe that it's impossible for me to catch a cold or that I should expect to live in splendor and excess from the cradle to the grave. However, I am convinced that God doesn't want me to be so sick and unable to pursue my destiny in life, nor do I believe He wants me to be tightfisted with my money out of fear that I might not have enough finances to take care of my own needs and the needs of my family.

The apostle Paul told us that God "redeemed us in order that the blessing given to Abraham might come to the Gentiles through Christ Jesus" (Galatians 3:14). And although the rest of that verse makes it clear that Paul was writing specifically about the blessing of the Holy Spirit, the truth remains that ALL of God's promises to Abraham were destined to be fully realized by those who would come to believe in Jesus. According to Paul, Christians are the beneficiaries of ALL the promises God made to Abraham. Because of the price that Jesus paid on the cross, all those who believe in Him, are heirs of the promises that God made to Abraham, the man who would unwittingly serve as our spiritual forefather.

Now that's important because God blessed Abraham in a lot of different ways. Most importantly, God blessed Abraham spiritually, declaring him to be the progenitor of the Messiah. But God also blessed Abraham with wealth. God made Abraham an independent and prosperous man in a time and place where that type of prosperity was rather rare. So, by today's standards, Abraham was well off. He was a blessed man—but he was blessed for a reason. He was blessed so that he could be a blessing to others (see Genesis 12:2). Consequently, "if you belong to Christ, then you are Abraham's seed, and heirs according to the promise" (Galatians 3:29), and part of that promise involves your financial wellbeing—at least enough to live and enough to give.

You may be asking yourself these questions. So how is God going to do this? How is He going to make me prosperous enough to live and to give? How is He going to make me financially secure enough to stop worrying about my finances all the time?

Well, He will do it for you the same way He did it for me and the same way He did it for Abraham. Most of Abraham's wealth flowed to him through the hands of other people. His riches flowed to him through the hands of unbelievers like Pharaoh (see Genesis 12:16) and Abimelech (see Genesis 20:14-15). Did you get that? The Scriptures show us that wealth will flow to you through the hands of other people (see Luke 6:38). It will flow to you through parents, grandparents, employers, mentors, customers, clients, and other people that God places in your life to provide for you and enrich you, and God will give you the gifts, talents, wisdom, and experiences that you will need to bless those people and serve them in exchange for the material resources they pour into your life.

Is that the "formula" that God employs to bless His people materially? Not always! Sometimes, God may place a coin in the mouth of a fish to meet one of your immediate needs (see Matthew 17:24-27). Sometimes, He may remind you through miraculous intervention that He is in control of your life and your destiny. But most of the time, God will bless you by causing ordinary men and women to "give into your bosom" (Luke 6:38, KJV). Through the hands of the people whose paths you cross every day, He will provide you with salaries, raises, bonuses, contracts, sales, inheritances, and business opportunities.

> **IF WEALTH IS SO WRONG FOR CHRISTIANS, WHY WOULD GOD GIVE HIS PEOPLE THE POWER TO CREATE IT?**

Even if you prayed for it last night, you can't wait for money to fall out of a tree, hit you on the head, and make you rich. And discovering oil in your backyard probably won't make you rich. Likewise, you can't move directly from your blue-collar job at the factory to an executive position in Silicon Valley and expect to get rich. Most of the time, God will give you gifts, talents, knowledge, wisdom, understanding, opportunities, creativity, or experience that is so beneficial to other people they will be willing to reward you financially in exchange for it, and then God will providentially connect you to those people, so they can "transfer" their resources into your hands. Those people will feel as if they are getting the better end of the deal because of your excellent attitude of service toward them. In other words, serving others activates God's promise to give you the power to *create* wealth (see Deuteronomy 8:18). And this, in part, is how

He will confirm the promise that He made to you through your spiritual ancestor, Abraham.

If wealth is so wrong for Christians, why would God give His people the power to create it? If wealth is so wrong for Christians, why would God make prosperity a centerpiece of His covenant with Abraham and with all those who would eventually look to Abraham as their spiritual father (see Romans 4:16)? Wealth can't be wrong because, according to the Bible, it is a significant indicator (but not the only indicator) of God's blessings on a person's life.

GOD ALIGNS HIMSELF WITH ABUNDANCE

Now obviously, as I have explained, wealth can have a dark side. It can be a curse. Whenever we displace God and elevate money as a priority in our lives, we can end up destroying ourselves, and I've seen that happen with a lot of wealthy and prosperous people who fall head-over-heels in love with their money. But again, it's not the money itself that destroys them. Rather, it's "the love of money" (1 Timothy 6:10, KJV), and I'll continue to drive home that fundamental truth throughout the entirety of this book. Money becomes a problem in people's lives when those people start pursuing money for all the wrong reasons and thereby become willing to obtain it in all the wrong ways. They don't obtain it as a byproduct of God's blessing upon their lives and their work; they obtain it through worldly means that are designed to bring immediate gratification that is accompanied by guilt, stress, and potentially legal liabilities.

At the same time, however, there are a lot of unbelievers who genuinely prosper because they follow the principles of God's

Word for creating wealth without ever realizing that those principles came from God. These people increase in abundance, not because God looks upon their lives with favor, but because they have unwittingly chosen to activate the laws of God in their lives and thereby reap the ensuing benefits.

> **WEALTH IS NOT A BAD THING. WEALTH IS A GOOD THING, AND IT'S A GOD-THING.**

The laws of God are fixed and eternal. The "life principles" that are handed down to us through the pages of God's Word are ageless, unchanging, and indisputable. Wherever they are faithfully applied, they will work, and they will work for anyone who practices them. So, wealth is not a bad thing. Wealth is a good thing, and it's a God thing. It's our attitude toward wealth that can be a big problem. Money is not evil; it's just a tool. The Bible says a lot about it—we just don't want to talk about it. When you read the scriptures on generosity and money through the dysfunction of your heart, you end up projecting that onto the Word of God.

Our choices and behaviors in pursuing wealth can drive a wedge between us and the Lord.

In Psalm 112, the writer declares:

Blessed are those who fear the LORD, who find great delight in his commands. Their children will be mighty in the land; the generation of the upright will be blessed. Wealth and riches are in their houses, and their righteousness endures forever. —Psalm 112:1-3

God's blessings, therefore, extend beyond finances because money isn't the entirety of our lives, but His blessings *include* finances, which *are* an extremely important part of our lives. Your prosperity is an aspect of your life that God cares about and wants to enrich because it is the one aspect of your life that can touch everything else in either a positive or a negative way (depending on your attitude toward it). So, wealth is not a worldly thing, and it's not a device of the devil. Wealth is one of God's promised blessings for those who understand its true potential and for "those who fear the LORD."

The belief that money is destined to drive a wedge between a believer and his God is simply not scriptural. In fact, as I have already noted, many righteous men in the Bible were wealthy, and many wealthy men were also righteous. Joseph of Arimathea was one of those godly and prosperous men (see Matthew 27:57-60). Joseph had enough faith to align himself with Jesus on the day that Jesus was crucified, something that nobody else dared to do except for the apostle John, Mary Magdalene, and Mary, the mother of Jesus. So, Joseph was a bold and courageous man of faith, but he also had enough money to demand a favor from Pontius Pilate and purchase a mausoleum in the heart of metropolitan Jerusalem, where Jesus was eventually entombed. God had blessed Joseph because God would eventually need some of Joseph's wealth to achieve His divine purposes for humanity, and God knew that Joseph would be generous with his wealth when the time came for God to call for it. In other words, Joseph had enough to live and enough to give. He had enough to do what God called him to do on the darkest day in human history—the day when Jesus died.

> **GOD DOESN'T MIND IF I HAVE MONEY AS LONG AS MY MONEY DOESN'T HAVE ME.**

And so it is with all the prosperous men in the Bible—men like Abraham, Job, Joseph, and Solomon—because there's nothing wrong with wealth unless it is elevated above God in our hearts, and there's nothing wrong with wealth unless we withhold it from the One who gave it to us when He requires us to return a portion to Him. God doesn't mind if I have money as long as my money doesn't have me. He doesn't mind if I possess "things" if those "things" don't possess me. God doesn't mind our prosperity because He created it in the first place, and He created it specifically to bless His people and enrich their lives. That's just who He is.

God made man in His own image, and He made man in His own likeness (see Genesis 1:27; 5:1). But it is not God's "image" to barely squeak by in life, and it is not God's "likeness" to hang from a ledge by your fingertips over the bottomless chasm of possible bankruptcy and financial ruin. It *is* God's image to prosper (to do well in life), and it *is* God's likeness to "flourish" (Psalm 92:13). Abundance is "more than enough," not "barely enough" or "almost enough." It is at least enough to live and enough to give.

The nature of God's creation and the nature of God's creative acts in the book of Genesis are meant to serve as reflections of the nature of God Himself. And when God created the world, He didn't hold back. He didn't limit, restrict, or "ration" the things that He made. When He created the first animals, for example, He "blessed them" and afterward said to them, "Be fruitful and increase in number and FILL the water in the seas, and let the birds INCREASE on the earth" (Genesis 1:22-23, emphases mine). He said this because He is a God of plenty, not a God of scarcity. He is the God of abundance, not the God of dearth. So how in the world can a sincere believer read the Bible and think that God wants His people to live in poverty . . . or even deficiency?

During the six days of creation, God also caused the land to produce "vegetation: plants bearing seed according to their kinds and trees bearing fruit with seed in it according to their kinds" (Genesis 1:12). Have you ever looked inside a watermelon, cantaloupe, or papaya? Take a few minutes and look inside any piece of fruit you might have in your house—an apple, an orange, or even a lemon. I think you'll get the point. God didn't just put one or two little seeds inside that piece of fruit and hope that the harvesters would carefully handle those few seeds He provided for them. No! God packed each piece of fruit with enough seeds to produce a harvest that could fill a warehouse.

I'm told that a typical papaya contains about five hundred seeds. According to the online publication *The Spruce*, "a single supermarket papaya will yield several hundred black seeds. Plants grown from seeds will sprout in about two weeks and grow to flowering maturity in just five to six months. Unless pruned, many varieties will reach the ceiling before a year has passed."[1] In other words, just one of those little papaya seeds can produce a papaya plant that reaches the ceiling of your house in less than a year, producing enormous numbers of additional papayas, each of which contains hundreds of additional seeds. So one tiny papaya seed can produce so many papayas and so many more papaya seeds that it would be virtually impossible to count them because God hasn't supplied His creation with barely enough to scrape by; He has packed His creation with abundance beyond our comprehension.

Then, when it came time to create man, God went a little further. Not only did God supply man with an abundance of everything he could ever need or want, but He also handed man dominion over all the other things He had made. In other words, He gave man ownership and management and accessibility to all these things without limitation or restraint (except for one forbidden tree). He gave all of this to Adam and, by design, to all of Adam's descendants after him . . . until sin eventually added burdens and hardships to obtaining this abundance.

> **IF GOD DIDN'T MAKE ALL THIS ABUNDANCE FOR HIS PEOPLE, THEN FOR WHOM DID HE MAKE IT?**

---

1 Jon Vanzile, "How to Grow Papaya Indoors," *The Spruce*, 25 Feb. 2022, https://www.thespruce.com/grow-papaya-indoors-1902490.

But the lesson we can learn from all of this is that God doesn't want us to barely squeak by. He doesn't want us to have to live off others to keep our heads above water. God isn't the God of "barely enough." He is the God of "richness." He is the God of abundance. And if God didn't make all this abundance for His people, then for whom did He make it? Did He make it for Himself? No, God doesn't need money to spend or food to eat. Did He make it for the animals? Well, perhaps to some degree, but the animals don't need gold, and they don't need excess wealth that they can share with other animals going through difficult times. Did He make it for Satan and for all the evil people He knew would eventually serve Satan's purposes in the world? I don't think so. Why would God want to incentivize sin and rebellion?

God made wealth for His people because God is a giving God. "For God so loved the world, that he GAVE" (John 3:16, KJV, emphasis added). God demonstrates His love toward us by what He *gives* to us. He gave us His best when He gave us Jesus, and He has given us the best of His creation for our pleasure, sustenance, and delight. But for some reason, a lot of Christians just don't want to believe that. They find it too good to be true. But if you really think about it, giving the life of His Son as a ransom for our sins is also too good to be true . . . and yet it *is* true.

God created a world of abundance—abundant with life (see Genesis 1:20), abundant with beauty (see Genesis 2:9), abundant with food (see Genesis 2:9), and abundant with wealth (see Genesis 2:11)—and He declared all this abundance to be "very good" (Genesis 1:31). What's more, He made all these abundant blessings for man and appointed man to rule over them. He made man for His pleasure and His glory, but He made everything else for man's sustenance and delight so that men and women would have all the resources they would ever need to live "rich" and meaningful lives, to fulfill their God-given purposes in the world, and to help others achieve the same level of fulfillment. Yet while man unfortunately lost his birthright to all these blessings when he forfeited them at the tree of the knowledge of good and evil, God has negated the curse that he placed on Adam and has replaced that curse with the blessing that is available to us through Christ Jesus.

PROSPERITY ISN'T AUTOMATIC

Understand that prosperity isn't automatic for the believer. Just because you're a Christian doesn't mean you're guaranteed success and great wealth. Jesus took our sins and our poverty upon Himself so that the curse God placed on the creation in response to Adam's sin could be broken and lifted from our lives. This means that we are now free from God's curse. But to benefit from God's blessings, we need to believe, embrace, and apply the principles He has given to us for our prosperity. These principles won't become realities in our lives just because they are written in the Bible or because we prayed the sinner's prayer of faith. For a specific promise to take root in our lives and produce fruit, we must know that promise and believe it, and we have to meet God's conditions for receiving it.

> # I SHOULDN'T GIVE TO GET. RATHER, I SHOULD GET TO GIVE.

Jesus earned the right for us to reclaim the wealth and abundance that Satan stole from Adam in the Garden of Eden, but we have to consistently live by the prerequisites God handed down to us for receiving His promises if we are to take hold of that right and make it a reality. If we faithfully follow God's required conditions for financial blessing, Psalm 84:11 tells us that God will not withhold any good thing from us. In fact, He "daily loads us *with benefits*" (Psalm 68:19, NKJV). But if we neglect to faithfully follow God's prerequisites for one of His specific promises, especially a promise that pertains to our finances, we cannot expect to receive the benefits of that promise in our daily lives.

I'm not a "prosperity preacher." I don't believe that prosperity is automatic or given for mere comfort or pleasure or because we simply "confess" it to be ours. I prefer to think of myself as a "generosity preacher" because I believe that there is always a purpose behind God-given prosperity and, as a spiritual descendant of Abraham, I believe that I am blessed to be a blessing to others.

I shouldn't *give* to *get*. Rather, I should *get* in order to *give*—give to my calling, give to my family, give to my church, give to the work of God around the world, give to other people who are in need, and give to the maintenance of a personal lifestyle that is void of undue stress and commensurate with my destiny, because the nature of God is not a nature of scarcity, and it's not a nature of inadequacy.

<u>The nature of God is a nature of abundance, of richness, of plenty, and of more than enough.</u>

CHAPTER 3

CREATE THE RIGHT MINDSET

We have been dealing with your belief system—those limiting beliefs and the beliefs you have about God and His nature. Our beliefs and mindsets are the foundation for everything in this book. This is the foundation for everything God wants to say to us about our finances. As we search the Scriptures, we see numerous principles of finance and economics, but the successful application of these principles begins with our own thinking. It begins with a mindset of faith that is capable of grasping, believing, and embracing the principles that God has revealed to us in the Scriptures. **The right mindset can bring us success; the wrong mindset can bring us misery**. So, the challenge that awaits us is the challenge of navigating a rather narrow road—the road that winds between our natural tendency to doubt that God will do for us what He has done for others, and the unnatural tendency to just accept every teaching about money that self-proclaimed "theology experts" offer us.

TWO ROADS, TWO DIFFERENT DESTINATIONS

Do you remember when Jesus taught the masses about the narrow road that leads to life? In the Sermon on the Mount, Jesus contrasted the broad road that leads to destruction with the narrow road that leads to life (see Matthew 7:13-14). He talked about the broad road that most people will travel in life with the narrow road that few people will ever find. Well, that narrow road is a road that concerns a person's finances as well as the rest of his life, and the sad reality is that few people will ever find that narrow road. Few people will ever find righteousness or real prosperity because they listen to the wrong voices, develop the wrong kinds of values, and habituate the wrong kind of thinking in their lives that will end up taking them where most people end up—on a broad and heavily traveled road to mediocrity, lack, and discontentment.

What voices have you been listening to? Those voices have helped to shape your values and your thinking. Let me just reiterate something I often say to those individuals I coach: you should never take advice from someone who hasn't been where you want to go or isn't where you want to be. When I was writing my book *The 12 Traits of the Greats*,[2] I studied great men and women and what made them different from others. One of the common threads I found in each of their lives is who they allowed in their inner circles, who they listened to, and who they let influence them. I travel all over the world speaking and coaching. People will hear me speak and then follow me on social media. Now granted, I don't put everything on social

---

2 Dave Martin, *The 12 Traits of the Greats: Mastering the Qualities of Uncommon Achievers* (Tulsa, OK: Harrison House Publishers, March 10, 2020).

media, but if you follow me long enough, you will most definitely get some good laughs, and you may just pick up some wisdom along the way, too.

A young entrepreneur named John who had been at one of my conferences started following me on social media and reached out to see if I would mentor him. So, I began coaching him.

He had always been driven, but for a while, he felt like he was stuck in the same place, not making much progress. His business was doing okay, his relationships were fine, but deep down, he knew there was more. He wanted to go from "okay" to thriving. He wanted to drastically increase his income, but he couldn't figure out how.

He asked if we could meet over a cup of coffee. John decided to open up. "Dr. Dave, I just don't get it," John said, looking a bit frustrated. "I've been doing all the right things. I'm working hard, staying disciplined, but I feel like I'm just ... stagnant. It's like I've hit a ceiling, and I can't figure out how to break through."

I leaned back, thoughtfully nodding. "I get that. I've been there myself," I said. "But here's something that I realized a long time ago and it changed everything for me." I looked John squarely in the eyes. "I realized that if you want to grow, you have to surround yourself with people who are doing better than you. Always."

John furrowed his brow. "But isn't that intimidating? What if I can't keep up? What if I bother them?"

"That's the whole point!" I said. "Think about it this way. If you're the smartest person in the room, how are you supposed to learn anything new? If you're the best person in your circle, how do you get better than you already are? If you surround yourself with those who never achieve more than you have achieved, you'll stay in your comfort zone. But when you're around people who are further ahead of you—financially, spiritually, mentally—they challenge you. They push you to think bigger, to stretch yourself in ways you never thought possible."

John thought about that for a moment. He'd always heard the scriptural principle that "iron sharpens iron," but he hadn't truly applied it. He realized he'd been comfortable, maybe even a little too comfortable, being the most successful person in his close circle of friends.

"So, you're saying I need to find new people to learn from?" John asked.

"Exactly," I nodded. "Find people who are excelling in areas where you want to grow and learn from them. Whether it's business, leadership, or even personal growth, never stop learning. Never stop seeking out those who are further ahead. I did that, and it changed the trajectory of my life."

> **SURROUND YOURSELF WITH THOSE WHO CHALLENGE YOU, AND YOU'LL NEVER STOP BECOMING THE BEST VERSION OF YOURSELF.**

Over the next few weeks, John committed to regular coaching and mentoring. He set aside time to learn what I did and how I did it. He asked questions; he went to speaking engagements with me and listened to every word I said. He attended my roundtables and joined mastermind groups. He even reached out to a few other leaders he admired. Slowly, he noticed a shift. His mindset expanded, his goals became bolder, and soon, he was breaking through the ceiling he had once thought was impossible to crack.

I gave John the key to continuous growth: surround yourself with those who challenge you, and you'll never stop becoming the best version of yourself. If you want to be debt free, find people who are debt-free. If you want to grow your business, find people with a business that looks like the one you want to have. If you want to operate within God's economy and not this world's economy, surround yourself with exceptional people, study this book, adopt the principles within the Scriptures, and let them guide you to financial success.

THE NARROW ROAD

The road to success in any godly venture will always be a road that is sparsely traveled, and it will always be a road that is "narrow." In other words, that road will be tight and restricted, and there won't be a lot of room on that road to veer off course. Fixed, eternal, and nonnegotiable principles will dictate the way forward that will eventually lead to life, success, and prosperity. However, because that road isn't wide, it won't offer a lot of room for variable thinking or optional behavior. It won't offer a lot of room for contrary opinions or opposing attitudes. It will be "narrow"—and it will be much less traveled. The good news is that this road will eventually take you to any godly goal that your heart can imagine. The bad news is that it's always easy to veer off this narrow road into a "ditch" on one side of the road or the other—the right-hand side or the left-hand side. Consequently, the challenge for the narrow road traveler is to remain in the middle, to avoid the extremes, and to stay the course of constant reliance on the eternal principles of God that will eventually lead to the realization of all His promises in the Bible.

When we walk with God down that narrow road of trust in His promises and reliance upon His Word, He will walk with us and help us along the way, and He will stay close to us whenever that road takes us through some unpleasant places. In fact, God walked with Shadrach, Meshach, and Abednego when their narrow road led them to the fiery furnace where King Nebuchadnezzar had sentenced them to die because they refused to bow down to his idol (see Daniel 3:1-30). This means that God will walk with you, too, when your narrow road takes you through trials that are designed to test your faith, purify your character, or better understand your true depth of commitment to the Lord.

> **IF YOU'RE THINKING IS RIGHT AND YOUR ATTITUDES ARE ALIGNED WITH GOD'S WORD, THEN GOD WILL BE "WITH" YOU FOR THE ENTIRETY OF YOUR JOURNEY.**

If your thinking is sound and your commitment to God's promises proves unshakable when those times of testing come, God will make sure that nothing—not even life's most horrific setbacks—deters you from the destiny He has ordained for your life. In fact, those trials and challenges will strengthen you. You will be strengthened in your determination to fight the good fight, you will be strengthened in your resolve to finish your course, and you will be strengthened in your decision to keep the faith (see 2 Timothy 4:7). But if your thinking is "wobbly" or unreliable when the heat begins to rise and you veer off that narrow road of firm faith and righteous living, times of testing will cause you to stumble and question the very essence of your relationship with the Lord.

If your thinking is right and your attitudes are aligned with God's Word, then God will be "with" you for the entirety of your journey. He will be "with" you in times of rejoicing, and He will be "with" you in times of upheaval and great turmoil. He will be "with" you in the fiery furnace of economic downturns, and He will be "with" you in the fearsome storms of financial need, all because you have firmly held onto His eternal principles as those principles pertain to your personal prosperity. You will have anchored yourself in biblical promises that never fail. The real estate market can collapse, the stock market can crash, and interest rates can soar, but when you are walking through that fire of testing with the Lord by your side, you will not perish in the flames. In fact, like Shadrach, Meshach, and Abednego, you won't even have the smell of smoke on you—because God will be "with" you.

What does it mean to you when you hear the word prosperity? Why do you want to prosper? What's driving you to want to understand God's economics? I would ask that we don't forget what we're really talking about. We're not talking about private jets, mansions, Rolls-Royces, and other material excesses of life; we're talking about the prosperity that God has promised to those who love Him and faithfully serve Him so we can "do well" (the actual meaning of the Hebrew word *prosper*) in all the important endeavors of life. We're talking about "doing well" as spouses, as parents, as professionals, and as supportive members of churches. We're talking about "doing well" when it comes to pursuing the purposes to which God has called us. So whenever I use the word "rich" to describe the way God wants us to live, it won't be to encourage you to start following in the footsteps of a Middle Eastern oil baron or an American rock star; I will be using that word and others like it to encourage you to pursue the "abundant" life that God has promised to all His faithful servants—the "abundant" life that will lead to sufficiency, personal fulfillment, and lower levels of stress. True prosperity and enrichment flow from a proper mentality toward money—a mentality that is neither love nor hate, but rather a balanced and "narrow" view of wealth through the prism of what God has called you to do with your life.

A CHANGED HEART LEADS TO A CHANGED MIND

Human nature is a strange thing that never fails to amaze me. In my years of ministry, I have met a lot of wealthy and successful people who feel guilty about the wealth they possess, and I have met a lot of poor people who tend to criticize and condemn the people who do have money. Even in the body of Christ, the age-old conflict between the "haves" and the "have nots" often comes into play because most Christians don't have a balanced and biblical view of money and, consequently, don't have the right attitude toward prosperity and the people who enjoy it. Wrong thinking always has been and always will be the greatest challenge for Christians when it comes to any meaningful area of their lives, money included, and that is why Paul said that the renewing of the mind must be a high priority for each believer (see Romans 12:2).

> **A PERSON NEEDS A NEW HEART BEFORE HE CAN HAVE A NEW MIND.**

Look at it this way: God can't really change a person's thinking until He first changes that person's heart because a person with a bad heart is never going to accept God or the truths that God conveys through His Word. A person needs a new heart before he can have a new mind. A person needs a heart that is full of God before he can start accepting God's thoughts and start thinking the way that God thinks. But the "heart" part of this equation is the easier part because God can change a person's heart in the blink of an eye while it can take Him a lifetime to really change that person's thinking.

In a single moment of time—when a person receives a revelation of his own sinfulness and of God's provision for him through Christ—God can change that person's heart and draw him to an altar of repentance and salvation. In a single moment of time, God can take a hard-hearted sinner like Saul of Tarsus and change him into a humble and anointed servant like the apostle Paul. But once the heart is made right with the Lord—often in a single encounter with God at the moment of conversion—then the difficult work begins, the work of changing that person's thinking; the work of changing that person's mind; the work of changing that person's deeply entrenched perceptions, habits, beliefs, and values; the work of changing that person's attitude toward everything that truly matters in life. This kind of change won't happen as quickly. The changes that God wants to make in a person's thinking are changes that will occur slowly, methodically, and incrementally over time. The work that God wants to do to change a person's thinking is a lifelong work and the primary task of the Holy Spirit, who, after salvation, finally has a foothold in that person's heart, so He can start the protracted work of renewing that person's mind.

> **UNTIL WE HAVE OUR THOUGHTS ABOUT MONEY RENEWED, OUR FINANCES WILL NEVER REALLY CHANGE.**

God can't change our minds until He first changes our hearts. Then, He can finally gain access to our minds and start the lifelong process of changing the way we think once He has changed our hearts through an encounter with Him at the cross. That's what Paul was talking about in Romans 12:2 when he said, "Do not conform to the pattern of this world, but be transformed by the renewing of your mind" (speaking directly to Christians). The primary work of God in the life of the believer is the work of changing or renewing that believer's thinking about every important subject under the sun and bringing that believer's thoughts into conformity with the thoughts of God as they are revealed to us in the pages of the Bible—and this includes God's thoughts about money. We need to have our thinking "renewed" when it comes to our finances. We need to have it "renewed" to align with the principles and promises that God's Word clearly explains. Until we have our thoughts about money renewed, our finances will never really change.

Think about this for a moment and you will see that I am right. Go back through time and think about your own salvation experience and spiritual growth since the day you were saved. How many things have you changed your mind about? How many of the old beliefs, attitudes, and perceptions that you embraced as a sinner have you been willing to set aside after discovering the surpassing wisdom of God's Word? Well, this "renewal" of your thinking is something that will continue until the day God calls you home. As He has done since the day you were saved, He will continue to reveal Himself to you incrementally throughout your earthly life and gradually change you as a person by changing the way you think about specific aspects of your life. To put it to you straight: you just won't think the same way you used to think before you knew Christ, and that's the whole point of this chapter.

Since the day God took possession of your heart at an altar of repentance, He has been at work in your life, revealing Himself to you and helping you change your thinking about almost everything you thought you knew. Now He wants to take another step forward and change the way you think about your money, and, as He has done so many times before, He wants to use His Word to change the mindset you may have adopted from your family, from a godless world, or from the erroneous teachings of a lot of well-intentioned Christians who have adversely influenced you. In a nation as financially blessed as the United States, poverty flows more from erroneous thinking than from anything else, erroneous thinking that is usually handed down to us from previous generations of our families and the people who have influenced us over the course of our lives.

What are the promises of God? What does His word say about the riches of the nations?

> **ALL THE PROMISES OF GOD SPEAK TO HIS ABUNDANCE, NOT HIS LIMITATIONS.**

Isaiah promised the Jewish people, "Your heart will throb and swell with joy; the wealth on the seas will be brought to you, to you the riches of the nations will come" (Isaiah 60:5), but God's people have to believe that the Lord wants to bless them before He will actually do so, and God's people have to position themselves to receive the Lord's blessings before those blessings will flow into their lives. Money can do a lot of great things for you. It can do a lot of great and positive things for your family, for the advancement of your God-given purpose in life, and for the kingdom of God through your generosity. But you must break the bonds of guilt and the mindsets of doubt or unworthiness before God's bounty can flow into your life. You must break the limitations of your own thinking that can lead you to believe that poverty is somehow God's will for you.

All the promises of God speak to His abundance, not our limitations. They speak to His power, not our weakness. God's promises point unanimously to the good things of life that He wants to bestow on His people, not the negative things. Read that again. Take some time to let that sink in. We need to speak from His perspective of abundance and power, not our limitations and weakness. This doesn't mean that every day will be perfect or that God won't allow some storms to invade our lives because the negative aspects of life are also promised to us in the Scriptures (see John 16:33). But it does mean that the normal posture of God's people should be a posture of bounty, not scarcity; joy, not sorrow; victory, not defeat. It means that the mindset I should have as a Christian is a mindset of inevitable triumph—the kind of triumph that includes my financial well-being.

Poverty will always be a reality in the world, and many Christians will experience poverty, as well. Jesus Himself said, "The poor you will always have with you" (Mark 14:7). But just because poverty is a universal reality and a reality that often affects Christians doesn't mean that I should embrace poverty as God's perpetual will for my life. It doesn't mean that I should seek to be poor. Rather, it means that people who are struggling with poverty are going to need my help, and I can only help those people if I have the resources to do something about their needs.

I cannot help the poor if I am numbered among them. If I am part of the problem, I cannot be part of the solution. So, I should learn to seek and expect God's financial blessings in my life, so I can respond to His tug on my heart to help those people, those churches, those ministries, and those believers at home and abroad who are praying that someone will reach out to help them. When God chooses to answer their prayers, He won't cause money to fall out of the sky and land on their heads. When God chooses to answer their prayers, He will do so through the hands of a person He has blessed with the resources that can change those people's lives (see Ephesians 4:28; Philippians 2:4; James 2:14-17).

EXTINGUISHING YOUR LIMITING BELIEFS

In 1865, William Booth founded the Salvation Army for the express purpose of helping the poor find Christ *and* regain their footing in life. Throughout the two-thousand-year history of the church, there have been countless others who have also responded to God's call to supply the needs of suffering people—needs like food, clothing, shelter, education, medical care, and basic transportation—and to do so for the same reason: to lift those people out of the depths of despair. But there are two important things we must never forget about the example of these selfless people and the admonition of the apostle Paul, who told us that, as Christians, we should always be willing to help those who are less fortunate than us (see Galatians 6:10). We must never forget that the purpose for rendering this help is to lift people OUT of the poverty that oppresses them. We do not simply provide people with handouts. It is God's will for people to thrive (to experience overall well-being or to prosper)—not merely to survive. We must also remember that nobody—not William Booth, not Mother Teresa, not the apostle Paul, not anyone—can meet the needs of those who are experiencing poverty and help turn their lives around unless someone with expendable wealth provides these noble ministers with the financial resources they will need to do their restorative work. Only those people who have hearts that are sensitive to God *and* resources that are available to God can fund these types of Christian ministries (note the example of Barnabas, who used his prosperity to help fund the early church in Acts 4:36-37).

Life will take us through seasons of excess and seasons of lack, and God will use both "seasons" to perfect us and to teach us to live by faith. In fact, Paul himself traveled this same winding road of sufficiency and deficiency, and he wrote candidly about the economic highs and lows of his life in Philippians 4:11-20. But the point Paul was trying to make is that there's no lasting spiritual benefit to either extreme; there's no lasting spiritual benefit to being rich or to being poor. The benefit lies in a person's ability to respond appropriately in faith to the circumstances he is facing while he waits for God's purposes to unfold in his life, and the benefit lies in a person's ability to do well and to prosper in other areas of his life whenever those resources are temporarily lacking. As we explore God's promises, you will see a recipe for complete supply and abundance. Consequently, as Paul explained to the Philippians, a true believer should be content in both seasons of his life—the season of sufficiency and the season of insufficiency—because an attitude of gratitude and a mindset of contentment will advance us in our spiritual growth while we wait for the tangible blessings from God that can help advance our lives and our life's work.

Your success in all aspects of life will boil down to your attitude, and, if you are a Christian, your success will boil down to the way you think about the principles of prosperity that are explained in God's Word and detailed later in this book. Because you are a Christian, you have already made your heart right with God. But now that your heart is responsive to the Lord and accessible to Him, He wants to do the same kind of transformative work in your mind. He wants to change your thinking, so it will reflect His thinking. Unfortunately, that process can take some time and effort because some of you have been heavily influenced by a lost and hopeless world tainting most of your thinking. You may have to break free from generations of misguided thinking that your family handed down to you. Modern culture may have taught you to think in ways that are contrary to the ways of God, and your family may have taught you to think in ways that are earthly-minded but spiritually flawed.

Therefore, while salvation (being made right with God) is an instantaneous event that will occur just once in your life, sanctification (growth in Christlikeness) is a process that will continue for the rest of your life. It is a slow and often painful process that will take place as you allow God to change your thinking through the power of His Word, through the direct influence of the Holy Spirit, through the impact of godly mentors, and through the hard lessons of life that the Lord will teach you as you engage the world around you. But this lifelong process is God's plan for you, so He can achieve one overriding purpose in your life: to bring you into conformity with His will and with His way of thinking (see Romans 8:29). God will not stop working to change your thinking until He completely recalibrates your attitudes so that your thoughts perfectly align with His thoughts, and your thoughts about finances are on the list of things that God wants to change.

I'm telling you this now, so you can prepare yourself for part 2, where the content becomes less theological and more practical. You will need to be able to start looking at money in a completely different way. You will need to see money and prosperity from God's perspective, not from the perspective of the world, which has been forced upon you since you were a child. Opening your mind to God's heavenly perspective on money is the only way you will understand, believe, and apply the biblical principles of economics laid out in this book because God's principles of finance won't align with the conventional wisdom of the world, and they won't align with the teachings of contemporary economists. It's going to take a whole new way of thinking if you hope to start living by the principles of prosperity that are revealed in Scripture.

> **GOD IS FAR MORE CONCERNED ABOUT CHANGING YOUR THINKING THAN HE IS ABOUT CHANGING YOUR CIRCUMSTANCES.**

Before you can move forward with your life financially, you need to break free from the kind of thinking that so often misleads God's people into believing that their faith and their finances should be separated or that holiness and prosperity are somehow mutually exclusive. You need to break free from the belief that the state of the economy, the status of the stock market, the current condition of interest rates, or any of the other "predictors of success" that unbelievers rely on every day as they make decisions about what to do with their money determines your financial well-being because God is far more concerned about changing your thinking than He is about changing your circumstances. He has already changed your heart, and you have seen the progressive unfolding of that change over the course of your life. Now, He wants to change your mind, so you can start thinking like Him instead of like the fiscal naysayers and short-sighted influencers who whisper in your ear every day.

RESETTING YOUR HARD DRIVE

If God doesn't want His people to have wealth, why did He take the treasure of the Egyptians and transfer it to the Israelites as they were preparing to flee the bonds of their slavery (see Exodus 12:35-36)?

If God doesn't want His people to prosper, why did He "brag" about the economic prosperity of Job and Solomon (see Job 1:1-3; 1 Kings 10:14-29)?

If God doesn't want His people to flourish and thrive, why did He provide Adam and Eve with gold before there was any real use for that gold?

God doesn't despise wealth the way that we have been taught to despise it. On the contrary, God created wealth, He blessed wealth, and He has frequently bestowed wealth upon those who have believed in Him and lived in harmony with His purposes. Consequently, we need to start viewing prosperity from a loftier point of view than the one an unbelieving world and ignorant but well-intentioned preachers have taught us. We must start viewing wealth as God's gift to His people—given to them, so they can have the resources they need to fulfill the purposes for which He created them. We must start viewing wealth as God's gift to us—so we can start walking in the shadow of His blessing and thereby become a blessing to others.

Abraham was one of the wealthiest people in the Bible (see Genesis 13:2), but there's a *reason* why God blessed Abraham in this way. God had told Abraham that one of the primary purposes for his life was to "BE a blessing" (Genesis 12:2). However, it's impossible to BE a blessing until you have been blessed yourself. Too often, we pray and ask God "to bless us." We ask

Him to supernaturally provide for our needs. We ask Him to supply us with the resources we need to pay our bills, provide for our families, or fulfill the calling He has placed on our lives. But God tells us clearly in the Bible that most of the resources He will provide for us over the course of our lives are resources that will flow to us through the hands of other people (see Luke 6:38, KJV). Those resources won't fall out of the sky, and they won't wash up on the seashore in a bottle. They will flow *to* us through the hands of the people God has already blessed, and they are then supposed to flow *from* us to other people in need according to the depths to which God has blessed us.

So if you want to BE a blessing to others, if you want to BE a conduit through which God builds His kingdom, and if you want to BE a faithful steward through whom God can change lives and meet the needs of others, you need to believe the Lord can prosper you, so you can pay that single mother's rent, pay for that little child's medical treatment, pay to dig a well for that church in Guatemala, or pay to distribute Bibles to believers who live in "closed" countries. You have to see yourself as a source of provision for others, but you can only do that after you have learned to see yourself as a steward who understands the true value and potential of the wealth that God can provide.

The things you have experienced in life and the things you have learned from unredeemed people have potentially distorted your mindset. Unfortunately, the knowledge derived from these two sources can often lead to self-inflicted poverty and a life where a negative mentality creates daily realities of scarcity and need. But the truth of God's Word can change your paradigm of life and wealth and "set you free" (John 8:32, ESV) from such bondage.

If you're struggling with a distorted view of God's financial plan for your life, you need to renew your mind. Align your thinking with God's thinking, so you will be able to embrace the numerous biblical promises regarding prosperity. You need to change the way you think about money if the world has led you to believe false or deficient things about God and His attitude toward wealth.

But what do I mean when I say that you need to "renew your mind"? If you can visualize your brain as a highly advanced computer, then I can explain this biblical concept to you from one simple analogy that will make the whole idea quite clear: You need to reprogram your computer (your brain). You need to wipe your hard drive clean, and you need to reload your mind with a whole new operating system and brand-new software that will provide you with new algorithms and new formulas for managing your personal finances. God's Word should be the "software" that you use to achieve this goal. You need to "delete" all the old financial files in your computer (your brain), and you need to replace those old files of worldly wisdom and past experience with new and "renewed" files that will enable you to align your fiscal thinking with the laws of God rather than the laws of man, which are imperfect, unreliable, and constantly changing. You need to reprogram your mind, starting with the most basic economic truth in the Bible—the truth that God wants you to prosper. In fact, He wants all His children to prosper. He wants all of us to advance and succeed in all the important aspects of our lives. And while God's providence may lead us periodically through some seasons of testing or into some unexpected battles or through some unforeseen storms, God's goal for our lives will be for us to "prosper in all things and be in health, just as your soul prospers" (3 John 1:2, NKJV).

God doesn't want us to live in poverty. He doesn't want us to live in scarcity or need. He doesn't want us to suffer. He doesn't want us to fail. How do I know these things? Because God's Word doesn't contain any promises or principles for bankruptcy or disappointment in life! God wants us to succeed, and He wants us to be happy, healthy, and able to support ourselves and our families while we fulfill the callings He has placed on our lives. Like any earthly father, He wants His children to flourish in all the meaningful aspects of their lives. However, the last five words of 3 John 1:2 should serve as our "qualifier" to God's written aspirations for us. "Just as your soul prospers" tells us that the Lord wants us to experience prosperity in our health, our wealth, and other aspects of our lives *in direct proportion* and *to the same extent* that our souls are prospering. And for our souls—our minds, our wills, and our emotions—to prosper, we will need to be transformed in our thinking. We will need to be transformed from a worldly system of reasoning to a godly system of reasoning, and we will need to do this so that we can understand and fully employ God's wisdom and His guidance for our daily lives.

GOD'S LAWS NEVER CHANGE

The world's laws, especially those laws relating to money, are constantly changing. The tax system, for example, changes from year to year. The deductions you took last year may not be deductible this year, and the percentages you are allowed to write off this year may not be the same next year. But God's laws are constant. Under the world's system, you can go to bed "legal" and wake up "illegal" because the world's laws are constantly fluctuating. But God's laws are fixed for all eternity. They will never change. So, if you want to be in alignment with God's thinking and God's laws and if you want to experience something different than you've experienced in the past with your finances, you are the one who will have to change. You are the one who will have to "bend" to come into conformity with God's way of thinking and God's way of doing things. You are the one who will have to change the way you make your money, manage your money, spend your money, and think about your money.

In heaven, prosperity won't be an issue because in heaven, prosperity will be "automatic." But prosperity will never be automatic on earth. Here on earth, there are things we need to do to receive God's promises and activate them in our lives, and the primary thing we will need to do is change the way we think about God's principles and God's laws. Almost always, the rationale of God runs contrary to the thinking of the world. So, if we intend to enjoy the benefits of God's promises in our lives, we are going to have to be willing to reshape our thinking, so it aligns with God's Word instead of the world. We are going to have to intentionally reject the logic of conventional earthly wisdom in favor of the loftier wisdom of God's eternal kingdom. And when we do that, we will prosper under God's promises to the precise degree to which we fill our hearts with His laws and live willingly in obedience to them.

From my perspective, the typical Christian seems to need only slight transformation in some areas of his life while he needs considerable transformation in other areas. In some areas of life, we tend to quickly and readily accept God's superior wisdom over the flawed wisdom of the world. But in other areas, we tend to get into a "rut" with our thinking. We tend to cling to the old habits of thought and behavior that we learned before we knew Christ, and these habits can often be difficult to break. I mention this because financial thinking seems to fall in this latter category for most Christians. For most Christians, their financial thinking seems to be one of those "sticky" issues of life that can be difficult for them to hand over to the Lord.

But here's the thing. If we decide to keep making our financial decisions on the basis of what we have done in the past or on the basis of how an unbelieving world has taught us to act, we will make the Word of God and the promises of God regarding our finances "of no effect" in our lives (see Mark 7:13, NKJV). But if we choose to faithfully do things God's way and to make our decisions based on what He has told us regarding our finances, we should soon discover that the promises of God are both genuine and reliable. As we realign our thoughts, our feelings, and our emotions (the three aspects of the soul) with the Word of God, we should progressively come to think, talk, and act more like the Lord himself—and the Lord never worries about shortages. He thinks and He has taught us to think that since "the Lord *is* my shepherd; I shall not want" (Psalm 23:1, NKJV).

In fact, as we continue to look at the Apostle Paul, in his letter to the believers in Ephesus, the apostle Paul conveyed this very same sentiment. In the fourth chapter of that letter, Paul directed the Ephesians to "no longer live as the Gentiles do, in the futility of their thinking" (Ephesians 4:17). Paul explained that the Gentiles (the unbelievers) are "darkened in their understanding and separated from the life of God because of the ignorance that is in them" (Ephesians 4:18). And Paul's simple, yet profound solution for the Ephesians' unrefined habits of thought was "to put off your old self" and put on the new self (Ephesians 4:22-23). In other words, Paul wanted the Ephesians, who had been steeped in the despicable thinking of their godless culture, to revamp their thinking and be completely "made new in the attitude of [their] minds" (Ephesians 4:23).

This everyday analogy of taking off old clothes and putting on new clothes enabled Paul to encourage the Ephesians to change their thinking by setting aside their former nature and seeking to be "renewed in the spirit of [their minds]" (Ephesians 4:23, NKJV). Paul wanted the believers in Ephesus to clean up all their warped thinking from the past, including their warped thinking about money, and to bring their thinking about every important aspect of their lives into perfect alignment with God's Word. In the same way, you should ask the Lord to give you "a checkup from the neck up" because too many Christians who profess faith in the Word of God live their lives trusting in the carnal reasoning they derived from carnal people who live in a carnal world to make their most important decisions (including their monetary decisions).

This is not to say that all earthly reasoning is faulty. Some earthly insights are quite reliable because they are based (often unintentionally) on the wisdom and the rich traditions of God's Word. But when it comes to life's most significant decisions, no Christian should ever base his conclusions solely on logic that people who are psychologically miserable, morally bankrupt, and spiritually lost blindly accept. God's people should look to a higher source of wisdom whenever they require guidance through life.

> **GOD'S PERSPECTIVE ON MONEY HAS LITTLE IN COMMON WITH THE LOGIC OF THE WORLD.**

King Solomon appropriately instructed us to "trust in the LORD with all your heart and lean not on your own understanding" (Proverbs 3:5-6). From God's perspective, therefore, leaning on your own reasoning and on the wisdom you have accumulated from your lifelong interactions with a fallen world is not the way to go. If you want to follow in the footsteps of Jesus and if you want to learn to think like God Himself, you will have to come to grips with the fact that God's perspective on things almost always stands in stark contrast to the world's perspective on things, and God's perspective on money has little in common with the logic of the world.

Learn to "put off" your old way of thinking and learn to put on your "God glasses," so you can see the important aspects of your life from God's point of view. As you strive to become more like Jesus, learn to hear things the way that God hears them, learn to view things the way that He sees them, and learn to trust that when worldly wisdom and divine wisdom clash on the battlefield of your mind, God's wisdom must always prevail. In the end, the world's wisdom will fail you and prove to be untrue. But unless and until you allow God to start the process of renewing your mind, you won't be able to see the actual depths of His wisdom or the absolute reliability of His eternal truths. You will be "stuck" in the rut of your old thinking, which works sometimes but usually falls short when it comes to its dependability as a foundation for a life of destiny.

God has not left you alone to figure things out by yourself. He has not dropped you into the boiling caldron of earthly life just to watch you struggle until you figure things out and get them right. God has provided you with a "handbook" that contains reliable solutions for all of life's problems. But until you possess a mind that can accept God's thoughts and trusting God's wisdom as it is revealed in the Bible, you won't be able to fully embrace God's solutions for your life—which means that His solutions won't work for you the way they are supposed to work. You will only see things from God's perspective, trust in God's ways, and apply time-tested solutions to life's most perplexing problems in a way that will testify persuasively to the people around you when you have a mind that is being renewed daily. You will be able to focus on actual solutions to your daily problems instead of feeling overwhelmed by them because you will know that God has already given you the perfect solution that will work.

Because you are human, you already know how to focus on your body. In fact, you do it without even thinking about it. Without even thinking about it, you know what your body needs—food, warmth, rest, or pain relief—but now I want you to learn how to focus on your mind. In the same way that you feed your body with bread, I want you to start feeding your mind with the "bread of life." I want you to feed your soul (your mind, your will, and your emotions) with eternal truths that can positively impact your spiritual, mental, emotional, relational, and professional health.

People who are self-motivated to work out every day, count every gram of fiber that they eat, and prepare their little plastic bags of carefully selected carbs, so they can bolster their physical energy have always fascinated me. The speed at which some people can learn not just the basic elements of nutrition but the specific and relatively unknown facts of nutritional health that can help them improve their quality of life has always intrigued me. But while I often come across people with this kind of fervor for bodily health, I rarely encounter anyone with the same passion for the nourishment of his own mind. I rarely meet the person who spends as much time in the Word of God as the nutritional enthusiasts spend reading *Prevention Magazine* or *Nutrition Today*.

Believers everywhere would agree that God has all the knowledge and all the resources He requires to meet all our earthly needs. But too many of God's children don't live in harmony with what they claim to believe. Too many of God's children are focused on inflation, gas prices, interest rates, and the latest unemployment figures rather than the promises of God. Fortunately, God's promises aren't dependent on the limitations of a manmade economic system. They aren't contingent on positive economic conditions. The modern believer, like believers of the past, lives "in" the world, but that doesn't mean that he should be "of" the world. As God's children, we should be living peaceful, healthy, joyful, and prosperous lives despite the less-than-positive economic conditions that exist in the world around us. Jesus has already paid the price for all the blessings that the Bible offers to us—blessings that aren't "automatic" while we are still here on the earth—but blessings we can certainly expect to see manifested in our lives to the extent we are willing to believe God's promises to us and obey the preconditions He has established for receiving them.

You can't put new wine into old wineskins (see Mark 2:22), and you can't put a new way of thinking about finances into an old paradigm of financial thought that an unbelieving world has fabricated. Allow God to transform your thinking, so you can start to think about money and every other vital aspect of your life the way He does. The principles of prosperity shared in this book should compel you, with the help of the Holy Spirit, to "stretch" and renew your mind.

CHAPTER 4

EXAMINE YOUR HEART

I've had a lot to say thus far about the role of the mind in a person's ability to believe God's promises and to meet the preconditions for activating those promises in his or her life. We have learned through God's Word that the world and heavily "marinated" godless logic have strongly influenced our minds, and this is why we need to "renew" our minds. As Christians, we need to start thinking less like the world and more like God because God's ways are almost always contrary to the ways of the world, His thinking is almost always opposed to the thinking of the world, and His laws almost always stand in stark contrast to the constantly changing laws of mankind and the conventional wisdom of unbelieving people.

But the Bible has a lot more to say about the heart than it says about the mind, and we have already seen that the heart needs to be renewed before the Holy Spirit can even gain meaningful access to our minds. To fully activate the promises of God in our lives, promises we will explore in the second half of this book, we need to understand the importance of renewing our hearts, because when our hearts are changed, our minds will be changed. In other words, in order to trust in the promises of prosperity and live by those promises, we will need to understand that believing the promises of God, embracing them, and activating them in our lives is more than just a "brain thing;" it's also a "heart thing."

"But what's the difference?" you might ask. Aren't renewing the heart and renewing the mind basically the same thing?

YOUR HEART GOVERNS YOUR LIFE

The mind and the heart are closely connected in the Scriptures, but there is a real difference. I have already explained how the heart can be changed in a moment of time. If you are a believer, you probably experienced this sudden change when you prayed the prayer of repentance and invited Jesus to become your Savior. But although your heart was changed quickly and permanently on that momentous day, it has taken you every day since then to start thinking in the ways that God thinks, and you've only just begun.

Another big difference between the mind and the heart is that the heart is typically more responsive to God than the mind, especially the unbelieving or unsanctified mind, yet the heart is notoriously fickle and can vacillate in its dedication and commitment. Why? Because, in the Bible, the heart is always associated with that aspect of human life that is responsible for feelings, desires, and decision-making, and all these facets of human nature are subject to day-by-day and even moment-by-moment change. So, in the Bible, references to the "heart" never refer to the muscle that beats inside a person's chest and pumps blood through his arteries and veins.

To the ancient reader of the biblical text, the word *heart* always referred to a person's feelings and passions, and all of us know how erratic and irrational those parts of us can be.

In the blink of an eye, due to some unexpected event, our feelings can swing from one extreme to another. Consequently, our desires can swing with our feelings, and our decisions will eventually follow our desires. That is why the Lord said, "The heart is deceitful above all things and beyond cure" (Jeremiah 17:9). So, the heart (the sensitive and impressionable decision-making part of us) is a little different from the mind (the part of us that accumulates data and generates more logical responses that are based on the information it processes). But the heart typically takes the lead in our lives and thereby supersedes the mind, at least during the initial stages of the decision-making process, making it necessary to take inventory of our hearts as well as our minds if we want to believe God's promises and satisfy His preconditions for receiving those promises.

Proverbs 23:7 tells us that as a man "thinketh in his heart, so is he" (KJV). It's not what the man thinks logically in his mind that controls his life; it's what he thinks and believes in the part of him that "feels" life and that "desires" certain things. The power that drives him finds its roots in the things that he really believes deep down inside on an emotional and experiential level, not a rational level.

That's why King Solomon, the wisest man who ever lived, could say, "Keep your heart with all diligence, for out of it SPRING the issues of life" (Proverbs 4:23, NKJV), and why David could say that a righteous man's heart "pumps God's Word like blood through his veins" (Psalm 37:31, MSG). David was known as "a man after his (God's) own heart" (1 Samuel 13:14, Acts 13:22), so he understood the importance of the heart in a person's life. He understood that it's impossible to live a life marked with God's favor without possessing a heart that is sold out to the Lord.

What you believe in your heart—the deepest part of your being—is what you will be. What you believe in your heart is what you will do in any given situation. What you believe in your heart is what you will choose as you face the inevitable decisions of life because your heart is where the promises of God will go to flourish or lie dormant, depending on the state of your soul.

YOUR HEART IS WHAT YOU FEED IT

When saturated with the Word of God, the heart can become the driving force behind a dynamic and powerful life. But the Word can't thoroughly transform you unless it first takes root in your life, and it is designed to take root in your heart first, not your mind. Consequently, you must do more than just "listen" to God's Word; you must "feast" on God's Word and "digest" it, so it can nourish your heart . . . and eventually reshape your mind.

> **THE WORD OF GOD WILL TAKE ROOT AND GROW WITHIN YOUR HEART ONLY TO THE EXTENT TO WHICH YOU FEED YOUR HEART WITH GOD'S WORD.**

If all you ever do is just *listen* to the Word of God, God's Word will never really change you. If all you ever do is just *listen* to the Word of God, God's Word will never produce much fruit in your life. Obviously, the process of spiritual rebirth and growth begins with *hearing* the Word of God (see Romans 10:17). But if you intend to make Jesus the Lord of your life, you must eventually move beyond the experience of merely hearing God's Word and start allowing God's Word to take root in your heart (see Galatians 5:22-23). Once God's Word has taken root and has started to produce some real changes in your heart and some real fruit in your life, you can start enjoying the rich blessings of God's promises on a significant level. But here's the key: the Word of God will take root and grow within your heart only to the extent to which you feed your heart with God's Word. You must hear God's Word to start the process of spiritual growth, but then you must learn to read and seriously meditate on God's Word so that the "fruit" His Word is designed to bear can grow in your life.

You see, the key to activating any of the laws or principles of God is to get them deep inside your heart because the heart is that part of you where you "feel," where you "experience," and where you "decide" what you will do, who you will be, and where you will go in life. Consequently, God wants you to meditate on His Word day and night (see Joshua 1:8). He wants you to continually fill your heart with His Word because the outcome of your life is irrevocably tied to the things you believe deep down inside—the part of you the Bible refers to as your "heart."

Meditation, unlike any other discipline in the Christian life, can cause the Word of God to flow down from your mind (the logical part of you that hears the Word of God) and take root in your heart (the "engine" of your life and the part of you that is capable of believing the Word of God). The problems that usually confound you won't defeat you any longer, and the temptations that usually overpower you won't conquer you any longer because the Word of the Lord is stored away in that part of you that "feels" and makes all your life-altering decisions.

Psalm 112:6 declares that "surely the righteous will never be shaken," and they won't be because the Word of God is permanently embedded in their hearts. They won't be afraid, and they won't fear bad news (like rising unemployment numbers, interest rates, or inflation) because their hearts will be filled with confidence due to the strong influence of God's Word. They will believe and trust the promises of God despite the ominous circumstances that may surround them.

So, God wants our hearts to be filled with His Word. He wants us to read His Word, know His Word, understand His Word, memorize His Word, and meditate on His Word, so we will be equipped to apply His Word to any challenge that confronts us and to any decision that awaits our actions. He wants us to be equipped to overcome any problem we may encounter in our lives.

Acts 19:20 (NKJV) informs us that, in the days of the early disciples, "the word of the Lord grew mightily and prevailed" (became strong and powerful). But God wants to see his Word grow and prevail with equal power right here in the 21st century. He wants His Word to be so strong and powerful in our hearts that we can face any foe who may oppose us or overcome any challenge that may hinder us, whether that challenge threatens our marriages, our health, our finances, or any other aspect of our lives. Our God does not want worry or fear to weaken and neutralize us. He wants us to be bold, courageous, and fortified for the challenges that await us in life.

Remember, God will always do His part in our lives whenever we are faced with one of life's great challenges. Whenever tremendous trials come our way, He will always fulfill the supernatural part of the victory equation. But God will rarely act on our behalf until we have fulfilled our own part of that equation, the natural part. God will keep His promises to us, including His promise to financially sustain us and prosper us over the course of our lives, but not until we first fulfill the prerequisites for that promise, and the most basic prerequisite for the promises of God is to get enough of God's Word in our hearts, so we will be prepared to fully trust Him in any situation we might encounter.

The prophet Nahum declared that "the Lord *is* good, a stronghold in the day of trouble" (Nahum 1:7, NKJV). Therefore, God is obviously on your side. He is "for" you, not "against" you. Even in "the day of trouble" (which will definitely arrive, even for the most righteous believer), God will be his stronghold when troubles come knocking at his door but only because the righteous man has committed to searching his heart and finding the relevant Scriptures that speak to his challenges and give him confidence that the Lord will bring him through. He will realize that the Lord will keep him and even promote him from the spiritual treasure of God's Word stored in his heart, even in the midst of life's most difficult ordeals.

YOUR TONGUE EXPOSES YOUR HEART

When the Word of God has been inscribed on your heart, it is a powerful force that can create faith and confidence in the most difficult times. But paying attention to the words that come out of our mouths is the only way we can know for sure what is in our hearts.

It is telling whether we trust God fully by the way we speak. I've heard people say things like, "Oh, I don't know if I could ever live in a house like that!" Well, you probably won't. When I tell people that one of my goals early in my life was to be able to give $100k to my church, some said, "I could never imagine giving $100,000 to my church!" They were right because they probably never had $100k to give. We have to not just align our hearts with what the Word of God says, but we must align our words with what God says.

We demonstrate our faith in God or our doubts about Him through the words that we habitually speak. We will know whether we really trust Him if we pay attention to the things we repetitively say. And if we have hidden doubts about God or His ability to guide the events of our lives, the words that come from our lips will expose whether we doubt Him.

> **OUR FAITH WON'T PRODUCE ANY CONSISTENT RESULTS FOR US IF THE WORDS WE SPEAK REGULARLY ARE CONTRARY TO THE THINGS WE PROFESS TO BELIEVE.**

Jesus said, "A good man brings good things out of the good stored up in him, and an evil man brings evil things out of the evil stored up in him" (Matthew 12:35). So that which is "stored" inside of us is bound to come out eventually, and the way it will come out of us is through our lips. That's why it's so important to pay attention to the hundreds of words that we utter each day, and that's why it's important to learn how to control both the number of words that we speak and the content of those words because, as James said, "If you do not [learn to] control your tongue, your religion is worthless and you deceive yourself" (James 1:26, GNT).

By failing to deal with the content of our hearts, which fuels the words of our lips, we make our faith "worthless" (empty, meaningless, and useless). According to James, our faith won't produce any consistent results for us if the words we speak regularly are contrary to the things we profess to believe. So, if your words don't match the things you believe in your head, then your heart isn't really "sold out" to those beliefs, and God's promises won't be fully activated in your life for healing, blessing, prosperity, or anything else until you deal with your heart and align your words with what you say you believe.

Remember, God is interested in your heart more than your mind, and your words reveal the condition of your heart. So you will be forced to deal with your heart, the fountain of either life or death for you and those around you, when you listen to your own words and work to control them.

The condition of our hearts and the words on our lips can promote or stifle any of God's promises to us. But since this book is focused on God's promises for our finances, let's direct our attention toward how our words can stymie the Bible's promises of financial blessing. It's sad, but a lot of people put themselves in "financial jail" and throw away the key because of the fear and doubt that flow constantly from their lips whenever they face a test or financial trial.

"I can't see any way out of this."
"If it's not one thing, it's another."
"The harder I work, the farther behind I get."
"I can't win for losing."
"How am I supposed to pay for this?"
"We can't afford that."
"Money doesn't grow on trees, you know."

What goes up must come down, but it's equally true that what goes in must come out. Whatever your heart is full of, that's what you will think about and meditate on. And whatever you think about and meditate on are the things that will eventually pour from your lips. Proverbs 6:2 says that it is easy to be "ensnared by the words of your mouth," so start paying attention to the words you repeatedly utter because, while your mind can deceive you into believing that you have no serious spiritual faults, your words can paint a very different picture of the true condition of your heart.

It's interesting to note that the word *confess* is an English derivative of two Latin words that mean "to acknowledge with intensive force." So, it's not *your* words that have the power to change your circumstances; it's *God's* words that have the power to change your circumstances and your life. Forcefully acknowledging your agreement with the Lord through *your* words has the power to "activate" God's words in your life.

However, your negative confessions can be just as forceful and hinder the manifestation of God's promises in your life.

God's promises are solid. They are sure, and they are available to anyone who will place his trust in them. While one man who constantly verbalizes worries and fears that deny those promises "neutralizes" God's promises in his life, another man believes God's promises in his heart and intensely acknowledges those promises through his words and activates God's promises in his own life. The person who realizes the promises of God in his life is the person who "intensely acknowledges" the things that God has already said to us through His written Word.

> **THE TONGUE IS DESIGNED TO "REGURGITATE" THE CONTENT OF THE HEART.**

Unfortunately, we will never be able to tame our tongues through simple willpower. James makes that fact abundantly clear to us. Changing the content of our hearts is the only way we can tame our tongues. I always smile whenever I read the analogy that James uses to help us understand this principle. He says that human beings have been able to tame just about every type of wild animal that lives on planet Earth (see James 3:7-8). We have been able to tame dogs, cats, elephants, pigs, lions, birds, mice, and even shrimp. But no man has ever been able to tame his own tongue because our tongues can't be tamed.

The tongue is designed to "regurgitate" the content of the heart. For this reason, we need to pay close attention to what we store in our hearts because their content will eventually become obvious through the words that we speak (and we won't be able to control ourselves). If we fill our hearts with garbage, garbage will flow from our lips. But if we fill our hearts with eternal truths, then those eternal truths will flow from our lips and will translate into fulfilled biblical promises. So, it's not a matter of "taming" the tongue; it's a matter of controlling what we feed our hearts and minds so that we may control the tongue.

Joshua 1:8 is the only verse in the Bible that uses the words *prosperous* and *successful* in the same sentence, and this powerful verse reiterates exactly what James explained in his epistle:

Keep this Book of the Law always on your lips; meditate on it day and night, so that you may be careful to do everything written in it. THEN . . . you will be prosperous. THEN . . . you will be successful.

Pay attention to the sequence. If you want to be prosperous and if you want to be successful, you must start by filling your heart with the Word of God, and you fill your heart with God's Word by meditating on it day and night and by speaking (confessing) the things you have read until they are solidly and permanently rooted in your soul.

God's Word is greater than any problem you could ever encounter. His Word is greater than any opposition you could ever face. But you must know God's Word before you can believe God's Word, and you must believe God's Word before you can draw upon God's Word. That's why the confession of God's Word is so essential to your success and prosperity. You will embed that Word in your heart when you repeatedly confess God's Word, and then your heart will guide your mind, which will in turn guide your life ... and success and prosperity will result.

So there's a real connection between the words that come out of my mouth and the level of prosperity I achieve in my life. If I believe God's promises to prosper me and if I meditate on those promises and confess them regularly through the words that I speak, the written promises of God are destined to change my attitudes, my behaviors, and the outcome of my life. But if I exhibit a lack of confidence in God's promises through my constant moaning, complaining, and blaming of others for the circumstances that surround me, then these types of negative confessions will serve as outright denials of God's promises to me. As a result, it will be impossible for me to consistently experience the blessings that my lips deny.

Obviously, it isn't easy to change this kind of behavior, especially when you've been speaking negative things every day for the entirety of your earthly life. It isn't easy to modify deep-seated habits of speech, and it isn't easy to alter the content of one's own heart. But it *is* possible! It won't happen overnight, and you're certainly going to make a few mistakes while you go through the process of reprogramming the hard drive of your own mind. But you can build a small "catalog" of the most powerful and personally impactful verses regarding God's promises to you that will change the focus of your thoughts and the content of your heart. Memorizing some of these verses, reviewing them at the beginning and end of each day, and learning to repetitively verbalize them until they become embedded in your heart and soul will change your attitudes, your behaviors, and even the words that you casually utter throughout the day. Then, when the going gets tough, these words of life will be there at your disposal to sustain you and give you a different perspective on the circumstances you are facing.

Several years ago, when I was on the verge of bankruptcy and facing the real possibility of losing my house to foreclosure, I didn't know what to do to solve this seemingly impossible problem. Even though I knew God's Word, I found myself going back to Philippians 4:13 over and over again, which states, "I can do all things through Christ who strengthens me" (NKJV). So, out of sheer desperation and with nowhere else to turn, I did something I had never done before. I just started reciting that verse out loud, and I would do that from the time I got up in the morning until the time I fell asleep at night. I don't know for sure how many times I would recite those words each day, but I'm sure it was hundreds of times. And I didn't just murmur the words under my breath; I enunciated them so I could hear my own voice.

As a result, something amazing happened to me. Faith started to build in my heart. I didn't know what was going to happen to me financially, and I didn't have any tangible reason to expect a favorable outcome to my situation. Nevertheless, faith started to grow in my heart, and God eventually came through for me in a miraculous way. So, when you are facing a crisis of immense proportions or when you find yourself stuck in neutral, making little progress toward God's destiny for your life, remember that your words will always reflect your true level of faith. What you allow to pass through your lips will be an audible expression of what you truly believe about God in your heart and about His ability to act on your behalf.

It's never easy to change your bad habits, especially bad habits of speech. But if you tend to habitually deny God's power or oppose God's Word, some real changes are needed in your life. Besides, positive changes in your speech can also generate some positive changes in your heart, your mind, and the circumstances surrounding your life. So, learn to "hold unswervingly to the hope [you] profess, for he who promised is faithful" (Hebrews 10:23). And if you should stumble as you attempt to learn this new approach to life, remember that the Lord will forgive you for the negative words you have spoken (see Hebrews 10:23). Then, get back up, dust yourself off, and continue the journey toward a new you and better outcomes. Continue memorizing and confessing the Word of God until you have built the kind of faith in your heart that won't allow you to settle for results that are less than what God has promised to you.

> **START SPEAKING VICTORY.**

God wants you to receive everything He has promised, so like I said, knowing what He promised is vital! God's will is always to prosper you—He will never forget you nor forsake you. So, when I didn't know what else to do, and it seemed there was nothing more I *could* do, I spoke faith. So start speaking faith today.

Start speaking victory. Begin today with these confessions for financial victory and declare them by faith!

- Abraham's BLESSING belongs to me. Abundance and prosperity are God's will for my life, so I call myself debt-free in Jesus' Name. I declare my mortgage, cars and debts are paid off. God's favor and BLESSING are active and operating in every area of my life (Galatians 3:14-29; Romans 13:8; Psalm 5:12).
- Everything I do prospers and succeeds. The wisdom of God helps me to make sound financial decisions. I am blessed and highly favored among men (Deuteronomy 30:9; Psalm 1:3).
- My God supplies all my needs according to His riches in glory. He is Jehovah Jireh—my Provider. My job is not my source. My credit cards and my relatives are not my source. God is my Source of supply, and I trust in Him (Philippians 4:19).
- I refuse to worry about my financial situation. I will not fall into the temptation to fear or have anxiety or any care. I cast my cares onto the Lord because if He takes care of the birds and flowers, He'll certainly take care of me (Matthew 6:25-34).
- I am a faithful tither—and because I tithe, my finances are protected from the devourer. I rebuke the devourer in the Name of Jesus—I command you to release my finances now and flee. I plead the blood of Jesus over my money and my possessions. No weapon formed against me, my family, or my finances will prosper in Jesus' Name (Malachi 3:10-11; Luke 18:12; Isaiah 54:17)!
- I seek first the kingdom of God; therefore, everything I need will be added to me. The Lord takes pleasure in my

prosperity, so I declare that I am prosperous in Jesus' Name! I have more than enough. I am blessed to be a blessing! I am a giver, and I receive a hundredfold return at this time (Matthew 6:33; Psalm 35:27; Mark 10:30).
- I walk in a spirit of self-control with my finances. I will not be tempted to overspend or lust after material possessions. I am a faithful steward of the finances God has blessed me with, and I will not go into debt from this day forward. I choose to live by faith (Galatians 5:16; Psalm 119:66; Hebrews 10:38).
- I delight myself in the Lord, and He gives me the desires of my heart (Psalm 37:4).
- I refuse to fear or be shaken by financial trials. I have the peace of God operating in my life, and I know God has a plan for me to experience financial victory in my life. I cast every situation over onto my God. He is my Provider, my Deliverer, and my Strong Tower. I will wait patiently in faith for the direction of the Holy Spirit. I am victorious in my finances (Isaiah 43:19; John 14:1; John 14:27; Hebrews 13:5; 2 Corinthians 2:14)!

Keep believing and declaring these confessions for financial victory, and you will see the manifestation of your words in your finances. No matter how troubling your situation, God can and will turn it around. He will make a way where there seems to be no way. Trust in Him, keep the faith, and stand and believe for your victory!

CHAPTER 5

SET YOUR PRIORITIES

Before we dive into some of the more practical aspects of God's promises of prosperity, I want to leave you with just one more spiritual principle that undergirds these promises because it's the spiritual principles behind God's promises that make those promises work in the real world. You will notice that each of the chapters of this book starts with an action. You must take action to create your own economy. If you follow these principles they will work for you. If you work God's Word, God's Word will work for you!

One of these key messages is that God's promises aren't "automatic." They don't belong to just anyone who can quote the verses. All the promises of God—each one of them—are given to us in the context of certain prerequisites. God's promises are real, and they are there in the pages of the Bible for everyone to read. But a lot of people find those promises difficult to believe because they seldom see those promises fulfilled in their own lives or the lives of other people. What they don't know, however, is that God's promises are being activated in few people's lives because few people are willing to fulfill the preconditions that God has established for their fulfillment. Any time that a person is willing to satisfy the prerequisites God has set forth for a specific promise of blessing, God will confirm that promise in the life of the one who dares to obey Him.

That is why I have taken some time upfront to explain the importance of one's mindset when approaching the promises of God. If we don't know and understand what God has actually promised to us in His written Word, if we don't have an understanding of God's nature and what His aspirations are for our lives, and if we don't have hearts and minds that can fully believe and trust in the things God has told us in the Bible, then none of God's promises will ever come to fruition in our lives. Our hearts and our minds must be right with God before we can fully realize His promises to us because the one common prerequisite that runs through all of God's biblical promises is the prerequisite of faith. Faith (total confidence in God's words and total reliance upon them) is the foundation for living a truly prosperous life, and that is why I have delayed addressing God's specific promises and the preconditions for receiving those promises until the second half of this book. That is why I have focused initially on the believer's thinking and the condition of his or her heart.

> **GOD NEVER BLESSES NOTHING. INSTEAD, HE ALWAYS BLESSES SOMETHING.**

Most Christians would like to live a blessed life, but many of them are apprehensive about totally trusting God with their finances, and many others have bad memories of their past experiences with some of the extreme teachings of prosperity. But if you fall in either of these categories, you probably suffered your past disappointments because of a lack of knowledge regarding God's preconditions for His blessings. If so, just remember this: remember that God never blesses *nothing*. That's right! God never blesses *nothing*. Instead, He always blesses *something*. You must do *something* before He will bless you. You have to do something that will manifest your faith or demonstrate your obedience to God before He will initiate any sort of divine intervention in your life. Even when it comes to salvation, which is a free and undeserved gift, we still must do something to receive that gift from God. We must believe. We must confess our sins, repent, and invite Jesus into our lives. The same principle applies to all of God's promises. God refuses to bless *nothing*. He always blesses *something*, and the good news is that He will tell us clearly what that "something" is. He will tell us precisely what the conditions are for receiving each of His biblical promises.

I have emphasized the importance of having a mind capable of believing God's promises and a heart capable of obeying God's commands, but there's one final quality we must possess to receive His promises: the willingness to put Him first in our lives.

BLESSED FOR A REASON

The reason that God blessed Job, Abraham, Isaac, David, and others is that these men never hesitated to put God first in their lives. All of them knew the Word of God to the extent it had been revealed to them, all of them had a firm grasp of God's true nature, all of them had a mindset of faith and genuine belief, and all of them possessed hearts that were sold out to the Lord. But the final quality that made them great and worthy candidates for God's financial blessing was the quality of having appropriate priorities in their lives. God was first and foremost in all their thoughts and decisions, and the thing that mattered to each of them most was the fulfillment of God's purposes in their lives.

For example, one of my favorite verses in the Bible is Genesis 22:3, where we are told that "early the next morning Abraham got up and . . . set out for the place God had told him about." Isolated from its context, this little verse might not say a lot to the reader of the biblical text. But the surrounding verses inform us that, on the night prior to Abraham's departure, God had spoken to Abraham and commanded this 115-year-old patriarch to take his son Isaac to Mount Moriah, where he was to offer him to the Lord. And this command, as harsh as it was, was made even more difficult by the fact that Isaac was more than just a son to Abraham. Isaac was the son God had promised to Abraham for a quarter of a century, the son who was born to Abraham and Sarah when they were both beyond the age of having another son who could take Isaac's place, the son who was the embodiment of all of God's promises to bless the world through Abraham's offspring.

Considering these facts, I am sure that Abraham didn't sleep well the night before his scheduled departure. In fact, I doubt that he even laid his head on his pillow. More than likely, he spent the night under the starlit sky, arguing with God, debating with God, and attempting to cut deals with God to change God's mind about this strange and painful command. But whether Abraham screamed at God, argued with God, or tried to bargain with God, the fact remains that "early the next morning Abraham got up and... set out for the place God had told him about" so that he could do the difficult thing that God had commanded him to do.

Now that's faith! That's putting God first. I don't know what Abraham did the night before he set out on his journey. Did he cry? Did he lift his clenched fist to the heavens and scream at the top of his lungs? Did he sit silently on the ground and slip into a deep depression? I don't know. And frankly, God doesn't want us to know what Abraham did to get through that night because all of us will take different paths to get through those nights when we are "wrestling" with God. But the one thing that God did want us to know about Abraham's response to this command is that "early the next morning, Abraham got up" and he went to the place God told him to go and he did what God told him to do. He went there without delay, and he went there with the definite intention of obeying the Lord's command.

Let me ask you: Why do you suppose that God blessed Abraham so bountifully? Why do you suppose that God prospered Abraham so tremendously? Why do you suppose that God elevated Abraham to such a lofty status in biblical history? It's obvious. Because Abraham put God first in his life... always! And that's the "secret sauce" for prosperity. If we have minds that think God's thoughts, if we have hearts that respond to God's voice when He speaks, and if we put God first in all aspects of our lives, He is bound by his own promises to prosper us and to promote us. And He will!

PUTTING GOD FIRST

What exactly does it mean to "put God first" in your life? In my opinion, it means precisely what it says. Putting God first means setting aside the FIRST DAY of each week to gather with other believers in the house of the Lord. Putting God first means devoting the FIRST PORTION of each day to the Lord with prayer and the Word of God. Putting God first means elevating the Lord above all your possessions (like that new Harley you just bought) and all your pursuits (like golf and pickleball). Putting God first means making God your first priority.

Many people honestly believe that they are putting God first in their lives even though their actions say otherwise. But we need to do more than simply accept Jesus as our Savior. To take the next step, we need to allow the Lord to sit on the throne of our lives, and when we do, true prosperity will follow because God will trust us with abundance as we no longer kneel to worship the things He has given to us. After Abraham refused to place his only son above the Lord, the Lord knew that he could trust Abraham completely, so God elevated Abraham to a status in human history that transcends anything that a twenty-first-century cultural icon could possibly imagine. But the point I want to drive home is WHY God did this for Abraham. God did this because Abraham believed God, he trusted God, and he elevated God to a status in his heart and life that transcended the status of anything else, including his own legacy and his most intimate and meaningful relationships.

In my experience, a lot of people believe they are putting God first when He occupies a much lower place in their lives. Oh, they've accepted Jesus into their hearts. That's for sure! Unfortunately, they've never allowed Him to be Lord over the most cherished aspects of their lives. But if we could all learn to get this one principle down, this principle of making Jesus first in our lives, the Bible tells us that this kind of humility and fear of the Lord will lead to "riches and honor and life" (Proverbs 22:4).

So again, there's nothing wrong with riches, just as there's nothing wrong with honor or life. All good things flow from the Lord. But whether we are talking about wealth or honor or life itself, the key to enjoying these things lies in *how* we have obtained them and *why* we have obtained them. Obtaining them from the Lord through humility and godly fear is the best way and the right way to receive any great blessing, but to obtain them in a way that relegates God to a lower status in our hearts and minds is to bring upon ourselves a certain type of curse that makes it difficult to keep these things and impossible to fully enjoy them.

King Uzziah of Judah was one of the good kings of the Old Testament. Unlike some of his predecessors and most of his successors, Uzziah "did what was right in the eyes of the LORD ... He sought God during the days of Zechariah, who instructed him in the fear of God" and "as long as he sought the LORD, God gave him success" (2 Chronicles 26:4-5).

If he sought the LORD, he prevailed on the battlefield, he prospered economically, and he grew in both power and fame. Regrettably, Uzziah eventually faltered in his faithfulness to

God, and he suffered accordingly. But "as long as he sought the LORD," his life was blessed in every way.

> **MONEY IS PHYSICAL, WHILE LOVE IS SPIRITUAL.**

Some people in the church believe that money is evil or at least unimportant because "money can't buy you love." And that's true. As I've already admitted, money can't buy love for anyone because money has its limitations. On the other hand, love can't buy you a house or a car or a root canal or a college education because love has its limitations too. Money is physical, while love is spiritual. But God made both the spiritual and the material worlds, and He has enriched us with blessings that flow from both realms. He also rules over both realms, so we need to thrive in both the spiritual and the physical worlds as the chosen beneficiaries of his abundance.

God cares about our spiritual lives, but He also cares about our physical and material lives. How do we know? Because God's Word addresses life from both perspectives! It offers principles for success in the physical world, as well as the spiritual world. While a lot of Christians tend to focus on one "world" to the near exclusion of the other, God's Word addresses both in a balanced way because God made both, He cares about both of them, and He has established the principles and laws of prosperity and success that govern both of them.

Is love more important than money? Of course, it is! As we have seen, without love, money is ultimately meaningless and will lead to ruin. Love is also eternal, while money is temporal in nature. But without money, we can't fully love the people God has placed in our lives while we are here in the present world because love is an action word, and money helps us turn our heartfelt feelings into practical actions in the "here and now." So, let's stop playing this silly game of "one or the other." It's both. And let's stop playing this silly game that pits the spiritual aspects of life against the physical parts of life because, regardless of how much love we may have for God, we still hope and pray that somebody with money will step up to pay for the new sanctuary we need, so we will have a place to worship the Lord.

I once knew a wealthy businessman who got saved and then said, "I don't want my money anymore." The knowledge of what he had done with his money before he came to know Christ oppressed him.

"God has obviously given you the ability to get wealth," I told him, "but now you have the opportunity to do great things for God that you couldn't do before you were saved."

"Well, I don't deserve all this money," he responded.

"Who does?" I asked. "God blesses us, so we can do His work and help others. He doesn't bless us because we're somehow worthy of more wealth than other people."

"Well, I'm just not interested in money anymore; I'm interested in serving God and helping people. I want to go to the mission field, and I want to impact people's lives."

"Really?" I countered. "Do you suppose that maybe God knew in advance that this day would come and that these desires would grip you? Do you suppose that God was supplying you in advance for something He knew would be part of your destiny? Before you were even born, God knew what it would take to fund the work that He wanted you to do for Him. If you didn't have all this money that God provided for you in anticipation of this day, you would be miserable because you would have a burden pulsing within your heart and no means to pursue it."

I encouraged him to stop feeling guilty or uncomfortable about his prosperity because now that he was a Christian, he could find a different purpose for his money. There is always a purpose for your prosperity. Once he understood this, he had the ability to solve a lot of problems for a lot of people, even people he had never met.

The fact of the matter is that it takes a lot of resources to fund God's work, no matter what form that work might assume, and that might be why some people are opposed or indifferent to money. Limiting our resources is one of the best ways Satan can limit the potential of our lives and our impact on the world. If he can delude us into believing that money is somehow evil, he can neutralize us or at least restrict our ability to do what God has called us to do. He can limit us as individuals, and he can limit churches and ministries throughout the world that depend on the faithfulness and generosity of people who have the means to support their work.

"Well, all I need is enough money to put food on my table and a roof over my head," one Christian man once told me. "I just need a car that can get me back and forth to work, nothing more than that."

"And that's one of the most shortsighted and selfish statements I've ever heard," I responded. "Here's a better idea: why don't you use your God-given talents to accumulate more than you need to survive, not so you can increase your own standard of living, but to give it away? Give it away to a missionary. Give it away to a single mom in your church who is trying to support three children without a husband or a decent job. Give it away to a young man who wants to go to Bible college to prepare for ministry but doesn't have the necessary resources. Just give it away or hold onto it until God shows you the greater purpose He has planned for your life, so you will have the resources to achieve it."

Remember our declarations? In God's Word we see His way of thinking, and it's clear that prosperity is always attached to one's destiny. It is always attached to God's purpose for a person's life. God blessed Abraham, not because Abraham was more righteous than everybody else in ancient biblical history, but because Abraham needed his wealth to fulfill the specific purpose to which God had called him. And, when Abraham demonstrated that he had his priorities in order, placing God's purposes for his life above his own desires, the Lord opened the floodgates of heaven and poured out upon Abraham not only wealth but a legacy that is unequaled in recorded history.

DISCOVER YOUR PURPOSE

And that brings me to a very probing question for every person who is reading this book: if you suddenly inherited several million dollars, what would you do with that money? Where would you put it, or where would you spend it? The answer to that question just might help you understand your current economic plight because God never blesses *nothing*; He blesses *something*. He never blesses inactivity; He blesses purposeful activity that is a response to His call upon a person's life. If you hope to prosper under God's favor, maybe you need to spend a little time discovering your purpose in life or better understanding it.

So many times we think it's about us when, really, it's about our purpose. God has made that clear to me again and again.

> **IT'S NOT ABOUT YOU. IT'S ABOUT GOD'S PLAN FOR YOU, HIS PURPOSE FOR YOU, AND HIS DESTINY FOR YOUR LIFE.**

It was a late afternoon, and I decided to grab some last-minute tickets and take my son, Solomon, to a baseball game. All we could get were some high seats in the top level, but we were excited to go anyway. We love major league baseball. As we were sitting there during the first inning, we noticed some empty seats way down in the very front next to the home team dugout. I said to him, "we need some favor to get those seats." We laughed about it and thought, *wouldn't that be awesome to sit there.* About halfway through the second inning I felt a tap on my shoulder, and a gentleman introduced himself to me. "My name is Steve, and I work for the owner of the Arizona

Diamondbacks. He happens to be here at the game tonight and has a couple extra seats and told me to come up and see if I can find some people who would be interested in sitting with him." Of course, we were definitely interested in sitting with him, so we said yes, grabbed our stuff, and began to follow Steve down some escalators and across the stadium, all the way to the exact seats that we had been pointing out a few minutes earlier. He introduced us to the owner, Jeff Royer, and he and his wife welcomed us. They said, "Anything that you want, just order it from that lady over there, and they'll put it on my tab." I could not believe this was happening. We thought, *Man, God's favor is all over us tonight. What a blessing. This is amazing.* After a few minutes, Jeff's wife turned around and said, "Are you all believers?" and I said, "Yes, as a matter of fact, we are believers." She said, "So are we; we are Jewish believers." As we began to talk, I told them about a friend of mine who is a pastor in Israel, Wayne Hilsden. They also owned some businesses in Israel, and Pastor Wayne happened to be one of their very close friends! We had a great time talking and connecting; they told us they had plenty of seats and to let them know if we wanted to come to the game anytime.

A couple of innings later they asked if we had ever sat right behind home plate and, of course, we had not. He said, "Do you see those two empty seats down there? You should go try them out; it's a pretty cool experience." So, his wife walked us down and introduced us to a man and his son. We sat down in the empty seats right next to them. Jeff's wife was correct. It was a pretty amazing experience. My son and their little boy talked, and his dad and I talked. I learned that his family used to own the Arizona Diamondbacks, and when they sold the team, they secured the four seats right behind home plate for life! We had just recently bought a place in Scottsdale, and so we exchanged numbers. He said, "We'll have to get the kids together sometime and have lunch, and I can show you around a little bit." I thought, *How awesome is that?* The two seats right beside theirs were available, so I knew we would be friends. It was an amazing night and an amazing experience. We met two new friends and, man, did we experience God's blessing that night!

The next day, I told the pastor of our church all about that amazing evening. He said, "Wait a minute, what did you say the guy's name was?" When I told him, he explained that their downtown location had been having parking issues. There was a parking garage directly across the street, and he had been trying to reach its owner for over a year. Well, you guessed it. The man that I met was the owner of that parking garage. I called Jeff and confirmed that he did, in fact, own the parking garage. Jeff confirmed that it wasn't used on Sundays and that if we needed it, we could use it. This whole time I thought, *God is really blessing me! His favor is all over me. He sure loves me.* It was all about me until I realized it wasn't about me at all. God wanted parking for His house—He just used me to accomplish it.

When God blesses you, He's got more than you in mind. I became a conduit of God's blessing for others. The blessings and prosperity that I received that day served a purpose beyond me, but they did serve a purpose, and it always will. I was just a conduit of God's blessings. How will you let God use you for a greater purpose?

I know of a church that, due to an unexpected blessing, was recently able to pay off all its debt, including the mortgage on its property. But instead of just sitting around after the payoff to rejoice in their newfound financial freedom, the church decided to initiate construction on a $7-million home for girls who had been rescued from the sex trafficking industry. Your prosperity is about more than just your beautiful home or new car or the amazing vacations you can take your family on. You have a greater purpose for your prosperity!

And that's what prosperity can do for us. It can give life to our visions and dreams. It's not about you. It's about God's plan for you, His purpose for you, and His destiny for your life. It's about His calling on your life. He gave you gifts, experiences, training, connections, and knowledge that are designed to position you for success in the work He has called you to do. All you need now are the resources. All you need now are the greenbacks that can turn your vision into a reality. If God hasn't given you a vision that requires great resources, perhaps He has given you the ability to gather those resources because He is planning to connect you at some point in your life with another person with a great and noble vision but no means to fulfill it.

PROSPERITY AND INDIVIDUAL PURPOSE

The first real visionary in the Bible was Moses. God took Moses to the top of Mount Sinai, and for forty days and forty nights, God poured into Moses a vision for a beautiful tabernacle where the presence of God could dwell among His people. God poured into Moses a vision for a priesthood that could represent the people to God and represent God to the people. And Moses spent almost six weeks in the presence of the Lord without food and without water so that God could explain to him every feature of the priesthood, every detail of the tabernacle, and every facet of the feasts, the offerings, the rites, and the implements and garments of worship that would have to be designed so that this remarkable vision could become a reality.

While Moses had every detail of that vision stored away in his heart and his mind, and while he had it all written down, he did not have the resources to make it a reality. He did not have the gold that would be needed to cover the altar of incense. He did not have the silver that would be needed to create the sockets that would hold the tabernacle together. He did not have the bronze, he did not have the precious jewels, and he did not have the fine linen and the other rare commodities that God told him he would need to turn his vision of a glorious tabernacle into a tangible structure.

But guess who *did* have all those resources? The Jewish people, who had just escaped slavery in Egypt! The crazy thing is that God provided them through the hands of the Egyptians, who gave the Israelites the resources they would need while the Israelites were fleeing their servitude in Egypt because God knew ahead of time that Moses would eventually require those things. There is nothing worse than an unfulfilled vision, especially a vision left unfulfilled due to a lack of needed resources. But for every vision that God gives, He also gives the necessary resources, and he usually gives those resources to somebody other than the visionary so that neither the visionary nor the contributor can take "credit" for the work. Only God can receive the glory by bringing these two separate entities together around a common passion for His work.

But just imagine for a moment what would have happened to Moses if the Israelites had refused to accept the bounty of the Egyptians when it was offered to them. What would have happened to Moses's vision if the Israelites had refused to accept the wealth of the Egyptians because they were convinced that all they needed was a tent for their family and a donkey that could carry their belongings? God wants to bless you financially either to fulfill a vision He has given to you or to supply you with the resources that can drive another person's vision to completion. But those resources won't do you any good and they won't do that visionary any good if you shun them, renounce them, despise them, or reject them.

This requires a heart and mind shift if you want to really step into the purpose God has for you and the vision He has for your prosperity. I can't think of a better example than my friends, Larry and Pam Winters. They didn't start off their life prosperous, but it sure has ended that way—in more ways than one. When they started their business, it began to do quite well. God blessed it because they understood it had a greater purpose. They shared that business with others who then also began to prosper. Over the years, the business continued to grow, and they knew that there was a greater plan than just to make a lot of money. They realize that they could use their business to not only help others do well in life but to share an even greater gift—Jesus. Talk about understanding purpose! Gradually, their business events grew from holding hundreds to thousands in their arenas to now tens of thousands of people. Their events give them an opportunity to grow and prosper, but also to receive the greatest gift of all—Jesus—the One who holds our prosperity.

I've had the opportunity many times to speak on those stages, share my testimony, and watch as hundreds and thousands of individuals made a decision to turn their lives around. Larry and Pam understand that their prosperity has a purpose. Not only have they helped others grow their businesses and populated heaven, but I have watched them give millions of dollars to advance God's kingdom through various ministries. If there were ever two people who understood how to create their own economy, live a generous life, and fulfill their purpose, it would be them.

What are you called to do? The resources that are needed to fuel every noble effort to expand God's kingdom are resources that will have to come from somewhere. Why not from you? So please, I beseech you, stop thinking so small. Stop thinking in ways that will limit your effectiveness in God's work. The Bible says that man was created to have dominion over the earth and all its resources (see Genesis 1:26, KJV), so be willing to accept some of those resources, so you can exercise your God-given dominion.

Here's another way to think about this subject: suppose you and I were driving down the street, you see a building for sale that would be perfect for advancing a vision that God had placed in your heart, and you say to me, "Dave, I would love to buy that building."

My question to you would probably be, "Well, what's preventing you from buying it?"

Most likely, you would say, "Money!"

And that's my point: money can't buy you love, and money can't buy God's forgiveness or His favor. But when it comes to a building, money can say, "I'll buy you." When it comes to a vision, money can say, "I'll fulfill you." And when it comes to a missionary in a foreign land, money can say, "I'll support you in your work." To poverty, it can say, "I will feed you." To opportunity, it can say, "I will accept you." As Solomon noted, "Money is the answer for everything" (Ecclesiastes 10:19)—at least for everything that exists in this present world. Without it, our capabilities are severely limited.

When we barely have enough to live, we can't say "yes" to any of the opportunities God places in front of us. We can't fulfill the purposes that God has given to us individually or collectively. So don't fear money and don't develop a negative attitude toward it. Money isn't a bad thing; it's an amazing thing and a blessing in the hands of the person who recognizes its divine origins and appreciates its positive capabilities.

After all, money can give you the ability to take dominion over those things that God has placed under your control. It can give you the ability to fulfill the purposes for which God has made you responsible. It can make you more of what you are. If you have any evil tendencies in your life, money will simply magnify and expand those evil tendencies. But if you have godly desires in your heart, money can help turn those desires into realities because money exposes everything that lies dormant in a person's heart. It can do nothing more and it can do nothing less because money is a neutral and indifferent resource that is designed to bring substance to the dreams and desires of the human being who holds that money in his hand.

I will never understand why the subject of prosperity has become such a divisive issue in the church when the Bible itself utilizes that word so frequently. David taught us that God's people should always be eager to say, "Let the LORD be magnified, Who has pleasure in the prosperity of His servant" (Psalm 35:27, NKJV). In addition, money is the mechanism that God typically utilizes to achieve His purposes in the world through the hands of those who love Him, and it is the primary "tool" that God makes available to His followers so that the man who trusts in Him can leave "an inheritance to his children's children" (Proverbs 13:22, NKJV). God is never disappointed when believers are doing well if their prosperity is helping to serve a greater purpose than merely to feed their own appetites or to satisfy their carnal desires. If you delight in watching your children prosper, know that God feels the same way toward you and all His children. It pleases Him when we are doing well in life, and numerous statements in the Bible establish that God wants His most devoted servants to "be prosperous and successful" (Joshua 1:8), not failures who are broke.

We must never forget, however, that prosperity and success aren't automatic, even for the sincerest believer. Prosperity and success are the direct result of deliberately applying God's Word to our lives. Yet, in the contemporary American church, the topic of prosperity is virtually taboo. At the very least, it is polarizing. Nonetheless, while this topic seems to confuse large swaths of the church, the Bible isn't confused at all. On hundreds of occasions, the Bible speaks boldly and directly to those aspects of life that pertain to money, and Jesus had more to say about money than any other topic except the topic of love. Besides, it only makes sense that the subject of prosperity should occupy such a prominent place in the biblical text because money can have a hold on people and impact society in ways that nothing else can. It can liberate and bless, but it can also destroy and curse. It all depends on what comes *first* in a person's life—his God or the money that God has entrusted to him.

PERSONAL CHECK-UP

Are you ready to take the next steps towards financial abundance and prosperity? I have spent the first half of this book helping you understand the importance of changing your heart, changing your thinking, and changing your mind. I have endeavored to help you understand how to shatter your limiting beliefs.

So, before you continue, I want you to take a moment to answer the following questions, because your belief in God's Word and your beliefs about money will shape your financial future either for the positive or for the negative.

- Have you shattered the limiting belief that poverty is a form of godliness? The Lord wants the best for you, and His best always involves more than just material satisfaction.
- Have you shattered the limiting belief that material wealth defines your prosperity? All the promises of God speak to His abundance, not His limitations. He wants to bless you in every area of your life.
- Have you shattered the limiting belief that money is evil? The love of money, not money itself, is the root of all evil. Wealth is not a bad thing. Wealth is a good thing, and it's a God thing. God wants you to have money if money doesn't have you. You are blessed to be a blessing.

Shattering these limiting beliefs requires a changed mind. Have you allowed God to change your heart and mind? If so, a changed heart will lead to a changed mind, and the right mindset can bring you success; the wrong mindset can bring you misery. If your thinking is right and your attitudes are aligned with God's Word, then the Word of God will take root and grow within your heart.

As I discussed, your faith won't produce any consistent results for you if the words you speak regularly are contrary to the things *you* profess to believe. The tongue is designed to "regurgitate" the content of the heart. **So, before you go any further,** start declaring these words.

"I am created in His image and have a unique purpose and destiny." —see Psalm 127:3

"Because I have made my choice to serve the Lord, I will continually increase more and more and my path will become brighter and brighter." —see Exodus 23:25/Matthew 6:31-33

"God richly supplies all my needs." —see Philippians 4:19

Watch your world transform as you align your thoughts with truth.

Now let's jump into the final half of this book and look at the practical steps you can take to see the overflow in your life!

CHAPTER 6

PAY YOUR TITHE

Many scriptural principles apply when we talk about changing our minds and hearts and understanding the nature of God that are foundational in these next few chapters. Now that you have assessed your heart and mind, I want to share with you what I believe is the master KEY to opening the windows of heaven over your life. God promises to bless us. The Bible is full of promises. But, every promise of God is attached to at least one prerequisite for its fulfillment in our lives. Happy (blessed) is he who is willing to satisfy that prerequisite through his unbridled obedience to it.

The new heart that God creates in me when I am born again compels me to do what the Lord has told me to do through His written Word. In addition, my personal experiences with God—experiences that remind me that His presence is more powerful when I obey and more convicting when I don't—compel me to want to do those things that please Him. Consequently, my new heart leaves me feeling unsatisfied in my walk with God unless I eventually start doing the things I know I ought to do (see Ezekiel 36:26-27).

I feel this way because God is the One who gives me the desire to obey Him (see Philippians 2:13), and the Spirit of God gives me the ability to understand God's Word to the extent that I can appreciate how true His words really are and how potent they really can be in this earthly life. In other words, whenever I am faced with a difficult choice in life and decide to obey the scriptures that I know, I will quickly come to see that there is a strong connection between my obedience and God's presence in my life and a strong correlation between my obedience and God's favor upon my life. I will quickly realize that obedient living opens the floodgates of blessing for me (see James 1:25).

There was an occasion during Jesus's earthly tenure when the Lord was ministering to a large group of people, and while He was speaking, someone told Him that His mother and brothers were outside the building, requesting to see Him (see Luke 8:19-21). Jesus responded, "My mother and brothers are those who hear God's Word and put it into practice" (Luke 8:21). So, obedience is the key to a thriving relationship with Christ, it is the key to activating God's covenant in one's life, and it is the key to receiving all of God's promises, including His promises regarding our finances. Obedience to God in any matter will directly affect whether His promises to us regarding that matter in our lives will materialize, so there is simply no other way to prosper under God than to obey Him in all things, especially those things that His Word defines as prerequisites for prosperity.

> *"Now, my son," [David said to Solomon as he was preparing his son to succeed him as king over Israel] "the LORD be with you, and may you have success and build*

the house of the LORD your God, as he said you would. May the LORD give you discretion and understanding . . . so that you may keep the law of the LORD your God. Then you will have success if you are careful to observe the decrees and laws that the LORD gave Moses for Israel." —1 Chronicles 22:11-13 (emphasis added)

Like all other scriptures mentioned in this chapter, The Bible is clear: We will live successful lives *if* we live obedient lives. We will prosper here on earth *if* we live the way God has told us to live and *if* we do the things God has told us to do. God promises to bless our finances.

But you shall remember [with profound respect] the LORD your God, for it is He who is giving you power to make wealth, that He may confirm His covenant which He swore (solemnly promised) to your fathers, as it is this day. —Deuteronomy 8:18 (AMP)

Additionally, 3 John 1:2 (AMP) says, "Beloved, I pray that in every way you may succeed and prosper and be in good health [physically], just as [I know] your soul prospers [spiritually]."

So, if you want your finances to be blessed, ask yourself whether you are obedient to God's Word concerning money.

I made my first million by the time I was thirty. There is no doubt in my mind that this came from obedience to God's Word and because I had purpose. I had prosperity for a purpose.

But it started with this one principle: my obedience to tithe. Obedience to the tithe was the master key that opened the windows of heaven for me. Stay with me; don't stop reading now! You may have preconceived notions about tithing, why we tithe, or why you don't tithe, but keep reading. I promise if you open your heart and mind to tithing, your life will be changed forever! The church should be the primary messenger of this important biblical law because the church is the primary beneficiary of this law. The church, according to both Scripture and tradition, is supposed to be the recipient of the believer's tithe. In my opinion, therefore, the seeds that we sow for the church should start with 10 percent of our income. Anything beyond that can be directed to those needs that the Lord lays on a giver's heart.

The people should give to their churches, and the churches should give to God's work in their respective communities and around the world. This means that God's plan for giving enables us to give TO the church and THROUGH the church to meet the needs of believers first, then others who are within the sphere of the church's influence. This is our formula for honoring the law of sowing and reaping in the church where I serve as pastor, and God has blessed us abundantly for adhering to it.

Still, a lot of people have asked me, "If I'm in debt, should I pay my tithe?" And the answer is yes, definitely! A financial advisor or accountant, steeped in worldly thinking, would probably tell you to get out of debt first so that you can afford to give because he or she would view your tithe strictly through the lens of tax law and worldly economics and would advise you accordingly. But the spiritual law in this situation must trump all federal and state laws because God will "expand" your seed if you will sow faithfully into His work. Give to Him, and He will give back to you (through the hands of other people) in a manner that will meet all your needs while you move incrementally toward prosperity. Besides, those debts are yours, not God's, so you need to use *your* money to pay your debts, not *God's* money.

In fact, that's how I got out of debt. I trusted God and obeyed Him with my giving, and He enabled me to pay off all my debts. At one point, I was heavily in debt, to the point that I felt like I had to reach up to touch the bottom. I couldn't get to the land of "extra" because I wasn't yet in the land of "even." But God enabled me to turn that around, and it's because I finally had fully committed myself to this principle of sowing and reaping, a principle I had been taught all my life.

I am a living witness to how a person can move from a life of lack to a life of "enough to live and enough to give." Meditating on God's economic laws, confessing God's economic laws out loud with my mouth, and acting on God's economic laws by tithing and giving extra to help meet the needs of others got me out of debt and prospered me. That's my own personal "debt-free program," a program that will work for anybody who dares to practice it and stick with it long enough so that the seeds that are sown into God's kingdom will have enough time to take root, grow, and produce the financial harvest that they are genetically preprogrammed to produce.

Let me ask you a question: who, in your opinion, thinks about money the most—poor people or rich people? You might think that rich people tend to think more about money, but the opposite is true. It's the poor people who are consumed with thoughts about money because they don't have any money, but they want it. This is another reason why tithing is so important. Tithing releases all our anxiety associated with monetary lack and propels us to give all that anxiety to the Lord so that He can become responsible for our well-being.

Stop worrying about money because worry won't produce a harvest in your life. Seeds that are sown into God's kingdom will produce a harvest for you because God's law of sowing and reaping always works. It works in the physical realm, it works in the relational realm, it works in the behavioral realm, and it works in the financial realm. Stop searching through the *Wall Street Journal* for your financial guidance. Search the Bible instead and learn what God has to say about wealth. Whether you're interested in investing, getting out of debt, or just basic money management, the principles for real and enduring success can be found in the Bible. If we take a step of faith and honestly follow God's requirements for financial prosperity, no financial problem will ever defeat us.

YOUR FIRST STEP FORWARD

Throughout the Bible, whenever there was a famine on the horizon, God would always prepare His people in advance. He would never leave them to fend for themselves. Now obviously, nobody can say for sure what is going to happen with our present economy. Nobody can say for certain whether there will be a recession, a depression, a recovery, or whatever. But this we know: for those who live according to God's principles, there is an assurance that the Lord will bring His people through any fire or any storm that may come their way. Nothing will catch Him off guard, and God will not allow those who have been faithful with their finances to suffer undue hardship when they have been willing to embrace all of God's laws and obey all of God's commands regarding their financial resources.

> **WE CAN DO FAR MORE IN LIFE WITH THE 90 PERCENT THAT HE HAS BLESSED THAN WE COULD EVER DO WITH THE 100 PERCENT THAT WE MANAGE IN OUR OWN STRENGTH AND WISDOM.**

I believe that God is the greatest economic genius of all time and the only perfect and all-knowing financial advisor. Whenever we follow His laws and His principles for giving our money and managing it, He will be there to inject us with all the wisdom we need to make good fiscal decisions, regardless of the economic challenges of our time. In addition, when we follow His principles and His laws—particularly the law of tithing—we will find that we can do far more in life with the 90 percent that He has blessed than we could ever do with the 100 percent that we manage in our own strength and wisdom. That's just a fact!

Unfortunately, one of the most difficult steps of faith for most people, especially in times of uncertainty, is to surrender any portion of their limited resources to God. But that's precisely when God wants us to do it. It makes complete sense if you think about it. No person can take a true step of faith unless that decision involves some type of risk, the kind of risk that an unbelieving person would never accept in his life. But God calls upon us to take huge steps of faith, so we can demonstrate our confidence in His Word. It's easy to give your money when money is abundant and no threats are staring you in the face, but it takes real faith to give your money whenever money is in short supply and dark clouds are gathering on the horizon. That's why God demands our financial faithfulness. It's one thing to *claim* you have faith in God; it's another thing altogether to have faith in God.

TITHING OPENS THE WINDOWS OF HEAVEN

If we don't release God's tithe back to Him, our faith is weak or completely nonexistent. In addition, God can't bless us unless we have empty hands that He can fill. If our hands are tightly gripping the portion of our wealth that rightly belongs to Him, He can't fill our hands with the additional wealth He wants to bestow on us. We're in a financial partnership with God. Our role in the partnership is to tithe, not tip, and God's role is to open the windows of heaven from above and rebuke the devourer here below. We simply cannot expect God to honor His promises to us in the second part of Malachi 3:10 if we aren't willing to honor our commitments to Him as they are described in the first part of Malachi 3:10. None of us should expect to reap bountifully if we are unwilling to sow bountifully.

The average Christian in America today gives less than $1,000 each year to the work of the Lord. So, according to the Bible, there are a lot of American Christians who are robbing God. But they're not just robbing God; they're robbing themselves as well because when we refuse to honor the Lord with our tithes, we rob ourselves of the opportunity for divine blessing. We rob ourselves of the opportunity to activate God's promises in our lives.

As a father, I love my son, and I love to bless my son. But when my son refuses to follow my instructions or to meet my most basic requirements for appropriate behavior, it makes it difficult for me to bless him. When he refuses to do his part to advance his own well-being, I know that blessing him harms him and reinforces his recklessness.

A person with a carnal mind or a natural mind (an un-renewed mind) just can't grasp the concept of tithing, and he never will grasp the concept of tithing because God doesn't think the way that we think. His ways are above our ways, and His thoughts are above our thoughts, and that's why His ways of doing things often confound mere mortals. That's also why a person needs to have faith to surrender to God's laws. God's laws don't make any sense to the natural mind. According to our reasoning, which requires no faith, tithing is foolish. According to our reasoning, if I'm having trouble paying my bills before I tithe, I certainly won't be able to pay them after I tithe. However, the opposite is true if a person tithes faithfully and with a cheerful heart because when we honor the Lord with our obedience, He always honors us, and He honors us because He knows how hard it is to defy the conventional wisdom of the world and to trust in Him completely. Our willingness to trust Him and to choose His ways over the ways of man deeply moves God. Our obedience deeply impacts Him. When we surrender to Him, He is bound by His own promises to provide for us.

This is why God invites us to test Him. "Test me in this," says the Lord (Malachi 3:10). Or, as they say in my home state of Mississippi, "I double dog dare you" to give it a try because in the end, trying it out for yourself is the only way you will ever know if tithing works. I'm a living testimony that tithing works, and so are millions of other believers around the world who tithe and prosper, often despite the bad economic conditions that surround them. But my experience and the experience of others isn't what you need. You need to try it for yourself so you can experience the power of this divine principle in your own life, and that's why I'm inviting you to accept God's "tithing challenge." If you will tithe faithfully and cheerfully for a reasonable period, tithing will become a powerful and reliable first step toward your prosperity. Few people truly prosper in life if they lack a generous spirit because generosity and tithing both require an enormous amount of faith, and faith is the "key" that calls forth God's involvement in our lives.

> **TITHING IS AN ACT OF OBEDIENCE, WHILE GIVING (ABOVE AND BEYOND THE TITHE) IS AN ACT OF FAITH.**

Despite how difficult it can be to tithe; tithing is just the starting point when it comes to a life of sowing and reaping. Tithing is the "bronze plan" for giving, the entry-level requirement for membership in God's "good and faithful" program of financial stewardship (see Matthew 25:23, KJV). After a person learns the benefits of tithing, that person will often start giving more than a mere tithe, and that is when prosperity really starts to manifest itself in that person's life.

You see, we aren't "giving" when we tithe because the tithe already belongs to the Lord (see Leviticus 27:30). We are giving whenever we start digging into the remaining 90 percent, which belongs to us. So tithing is an act of obedience while giving (above and beyond the tithe) is an act of faith. My tithe is a fixed amount (10 percent), but my level of faith determines my offerings, and that means that tithing will open the windows of heaven for me while my giving (above and beyond the tithe) will determine the size, scope, and frequency of the blessings that flow through those open windows.

I could just about write and speak on this subject *forever*, but let me add just one more thought, through my personal testimony, to this idea of sowing and reaping to help you make the connections between your giving and your potential for prosperity. When I was a young man, a student in college, I worked part-time at a UPS distribution center. And if I remember correctly, I was making about $170 each week. That's when I first heard about the "faith tithe." Somebody shared with me the idea of tithing on what I *wanted* to make instead of what I was making each week. So instead of tithing $17 per week, I started "faith tithing" $20 per week, which really amounts to a $17 tithe plus a $3 offering. After doing that faithfully for a while, I got a promotion, and I started making about $225 per week. Then I started "faith tithing" $25 per week ($22.50 for my tithe plus an offering of $2.50). Then I picked up another part-time job that paid me an additional $75 per week. So, this concept of tithing and giving is not just "theoretical." It's something I have experienced throughout my life, and it has never failed to work for me. I can testify to the fact that it's been my "above and beyond" giving that has opened the floodgates of blessing for me. "He who sows sparingly will also reap sparingly, and he who sows bountifully will also reap bountifully" (2 Corinthians 9:6, NKJV). You must put those seeds in the ground!

Here's my challenge to you: if you've never really tried to tithe for a reasonable stretch of time, start doing it now, and do it long enough to give God an honest opportunity to produce some real results in your life, at least for a year. No farmer plants his seeds and then harvests them the next day or the next week. A farmer must be patient, and he must work his fields and tend his crops after he plants them. So put your seed in the ground consistently and wait to see what happens. Then, after you see the divine benefits that tithing can produce in your life, take the next step and start giving God some offerings that are above and beyond your tithe. Exercise your faith incrementally; don't be stupid or presumptuous. At the same time, however, don't consume all your excess (that which remains after you have given to God). Instead, learn to sow some of that excess into God's work or into the lives of people who could benefit from your monetary contributions.

Remember, the farmer doesn't sow all his seeds, but he doesn't eat all his seeds either. He sets aside some seeds for consumption and other seeds for planting. So, you need to start with 10 percent and then move forward step by step as God enables you. In the same way that a hard workout can cause your muscles to ache if you're not used to it, giving too much too fast can cause a lot of financial discomfort. Stretch your faith and your giving capacity the same way you would stretch your muscles—a little bit at a time. Too many people have lost their faith and abandoned their desire to give because of presumptuous acts of giving that didn't go well.

Even if you're on a fixed income, take steps to obey God because God can provide for you in multiple ways, just as He provided for me in multiple ways when I was in college. After all, the question is really a simple one: do you believe God's Word and His promises to provide for you, or do you believe that those promises are false? If you believe that God's promises are true, then rest in the assurance that God has the power to take care of you.

The concept of prosperity is troublesome to a lot of us, but, as I have said, prosperity isn't about an increase in your standard of living. It's not about an increase in the size of your house or the number of cars in your driveway. It's about an increase that will enable you to support yourself at a level that is consistent with your occupation and calling, an increase that will allow you to adequately provide for your family and their needs and dreams, and an increase that will fill your purse with enough "seeds" to sow into worthy ministry activities and the lives of other people whom God wants you to "touch" on His behalf to change the circumstances of their lives. So be faithful to God so that He can be faithful to you and can place in your hands the resources that He wants you to make available to the work of His kingdom.

By now, you've probably seen enough scripture to know that the word *prosper* or prosperity appears over ninety times throughout the Bible. That's why I just can't understand why so many Christians have decided that the word *prosperity* should be struck from their vocabulary. We often read the Book of Acts and claim that we want to experience the same spiritual power that the early church experienced, including the power of the promised Holy Spirit. So why don't we desire God's promises of prosperity with that same zeal? Why do we seek one type of spiritual blessing from God while denying another type of promised blessing? I want all the blessings God has promised to those who love and obey Him. I want the promise of salvation, the promise of the Holy Spirit, the promise of eternal life, and the promise of divine prosperity in my earthly life.

Job 36:11 says, "If they obey and serve him, they will spend the rest of their days in prosperity and their years in contentment." And in 1 Kings 2:2-3, David tells Solomon,

> *"Be strong, act like a man, and observe what the LORD your God requires: Walk in obedience to him, and keep his decrees and commands, his laws and regulations, as written in the Law of Moses. Do this so that you may prosper in all you do and wherever you go."*

Then Solomon, later in life, encouraged his own son to keep the commands of God because "they will prolong your life many years and bring you peace and prosperity" (Proverbs 3:2).

Could the Bible be any clearer? Prosperity! Prosperity! Prosperity... *it is a resounding promise* that each of these verses has set forth *if* we will learn to obey the Lord by meeting the conditions for prosperity. So it's obvious to me: if I will read these scriptural passages and others like them, if I will believe them when I read them, if I will memorize them, so I can confess them daily, and if I will do what they tell me to do, I can expect God's blessings on every aspect of my life . . . and that, my friend, is the essence of prosperity.

> **WE FAIL TO OBEY GOD IN THEIR FINANCES BECAUSE THEY FAIL TO TRUST GOD WITH OUR FINANCES.**

However, I do understand why a lot of us fail to achieve the kind of prosperity that the Bible promises. We fail to achieve a wholly prosperous life because we fail to do the things God has told us to do in certain areas where we don't yet fully trust the Lord. Specifically, we fail to *obey God in* our finances because we fail to *trust God with* our finances. But if we will do what God has told us to do financially, He has promised us that we will "do well" with our finances, just as we "do well" in the other areas of our lives where we trust and obey Him.

It's up to you. You don't have to do what God has told you to do. You are a free agent, and you get to choose the kind of life you want to live. If you choose to disobey the Lord, He will never stop loving you, and He will never stop working in your heart to convince you of the superiority and the wisdom of His ways in those areas where you doubt Him. But if you do choose to obey Him, you can rest in the knowledge that your obedience will yield all the benefits of a blessed life that

God has promised to those who fully trust Him. So, the time has come to stop straddling the fence. The time has come to choose: disobedience with inevitable decline or obedience with divine prosperity.

CHAPTER 7

DETERMINE TO DO THE WORK

The promises of God are never "automatic" for anyone. It doesn't matter how sincerely you believe those promises. It doesn't matter how faithfully you confess them. It doesn't matter how often you read them, how enthusiastically you quote them, or how diligently you pray and fast to bring them to manifestation in your life. If you don't do what is required of you to meet the conditions that God has established as His prerequisites for those promises, you will never actually experience them for yourself.

This is especially true when it comes to the promises of God that pertain to prosperity. Prosperity is not "automatic" in the believer's life. Prosperity doesn't just "happen" because a person loves Jesus, and that is why so many godly people never know what it means to live with financial security. To experience the Bible's promises concerning prosperity, a person must be willing to believe those promises, but he or she must also be willing to obediently meet all the conditions that the Bible has established for activating those promises in the physical world.

That is why, to this point, we have placed so much emphasis on the biblical preconditions that relate to a person's thinking because what we *do* in life will flow from what we *believe* and what we *think*. What we do in everyday life will flow from a proper mindset, an accurate understanding of the nature of God, and a willingness to obey the Lord, even when we don't fully understand *why* He demands certain things from us. But now we need to start taking a closer look at some of the more practical prerequisites for prosperity, and I want to start with the prerequisite of a godly work ethic.

In the Bible—both the Old Testament and the New Testament—God teaches us the value of hard work, He teaches us about the benefits of a life that is defined by hard work, and He encourages us to develop and nurture the type of discipline that will motivate us to work hard throughout the course of our lives.

Some people believe that they can just *pray,* and God will open the floodgates of heaven for them and pour out His blessings upon their lives without measure. Others believe that they can simply *confess* the promises of God with conviction and authority, and the springs of financial abundance will erupt and overflow in their lives. Somehow, too many people have been taught to see God as glorified "genie," who exists to grant all their wishes and desires if they just believe the right things and say the right things out loud in the right way. And don't get me wrong: prayer and confession are important, but they are both completely impotent without the action of obedience. It is obedience that substantiates those prayers and confessions.

So, I'm here to tell you the truth about what the Bible clearly teaches, not just about the mental and spiritual preconditions for prosperity. I'm here to explain the practical, tangible, and behavioral preconditions for success and an abundant life because I want you to understand that you can pray until you have calluses on your knees and you can ask the elders of the church to lay their hands on you until they rub a bald spot on the top of your head, but until you become willing to actually *do* what it takes to meet God's preconditions for success in the physical world, you will never actually achieve financial prosperity. At the top of God's list of behavioral preconditions for prosperity is the willingness to work hard to provide for yourself and achieve your God-given goals.

THE ANATOMY OF A MIRACLE

If you read biblical accounts of any miracle Jesus performed during His earthly life, you will almost always find that some step of faith or visible action was required of the person in need of the miracle before they could see the miracle. You will find that Jesus asked the recipient to do something before He performed a miracle on that person's behalf. In fact, Jesus rarely honored a person's request to perform a miracle in that person's life unless the person first showed a willingness to do something for himself in an act of faith.

> **IF WE DO THE DIFFICULT PART, GOD WILL DO THE IMPOSSIBLE PART.**

For example, when Jesus turned water into wine in John 2 (His first recorded miracle), He waited for the servants to bring Him the pots and fill them with water before He performed the miracle they could not perform. When Peter wanted to walk on the water with Jesus in Matthew 14, Jesus required Peter to get out of the boat and take small steps on the water before the Lord was willing to reach out His hand and help Peter stay afloat. When Jesus blessed Peter and his fishing companions with the great catch in Luke 5, He didn't perform that miracle until Peter and his business partners obeyed His directive to physically row their boats out into the water once again after having spent the entire night fishing without success.

The principle here is a simple one: If we will do the physical and practical part of the miracle that we seek, God will do the spiritual part of that miracle. If we do the difficult part, God will do the impossible part. But if we won't take the most basic steps to help ourselves, God will not be obliged to help us in any way, despite our faith and our prayers. He will not become our personal genie—who grants our wishes because we have rubbed the magic lamp or recited the magical formula—and reinforce our laziness.

In Ephesians 6:13, the apostle Paul utilized one of the most powerful analogies in the Bible to strengthen the Ephesian believers in their struggle against a godless culture. Paul used the analogy of clothing oneself in the "armor of God" (the sword of the Spirit, the belt of truth, the breastplate of righteousness, the helmet of salvation, and feet fitted with readiness from the gospel of peace) to prevail against the spiritual forces that surround us. But as Paul encouraged the Ephesians to metaphorically clothe themselves for a spiritual battle against a godless world, he told them this: "And after you have done everything, to stand" (Ephesians 6:13). In other words, Paul wanted the Ephesians to do everything they could possibly do to "clothe" themselves in God's armor. He wanted them to do everything they could possibly do to defend themselves against spiritual attack, prepare themselves for conflict with a hostile world, and bolster themselves mentally, spiritually, and emotionally for a life that would invite opposition. After they had done everything, they could possibly do to sustain themselves in their stance against an evil world, Paul just wanted the Ephesians "to stand." He just wanted them to dig their heels into the dirt, resolve themselves to the idea that the world was never going to approve of their devotion to Christ, and refuse to budge in their commitment to the principles of their faith. So, Paul's injunction to them was simply "to stand" and to let God do the rest. Paul wanted the Ephesians to do everything they knew to do and everything they had the power and ability to do in their quest for spiritual security and then trust God to do the rest. And that is the formula for a genuine miracle. If we will simply show up for the battle and do our part of the equation that we can do, God will do the part of the equation that we cannot do.

The implication in Paul's injunction to the Ephesians is that God doesn't feel obligated or inclined to do miraculous things for people who won't take the simplest and most practical steps to help themselves. Unfortunately, too many of us fall into that category. Too many of us are simply unwilling to carry our own water or to "pick up [our] mat and walk" (John 5:8). Too many of us have been convinced that all we must do is "believe" something and "confess" it until it somehow becomes a reality in our lives. But nothing could be farther from the truth. There is always at least one precondition for every miracle and every promise of God in the Bible. There is always at least one requirement for us to *do something* for ourselves before God will *do something* on our behalf, and the most basic thing we can do for ourselves in the pursuit of financial security is work hard. Unless we demonstrate a willingness to work hard to advance our own lives and achieve our own dreams, the Lord will not be obliged to help us in any material way.

Do you understand the true purpose and nature of work? Some people believe that work was part of God's judgment against Adam. These people resent work, and they seem to be anxiously awaiting the day when they can go to heaven, so they won't ever have to work again. I'm not sure which Bible these people are reading because they certainly aren't reading the same Bible that I read every day. The Bible that I read tells me that work is a blessing. Work was something that God gave to Adam in the Garden of Eden *before* sin entered the world and *before* God cursed the ground (He never cursed Adam).

In the beginning, when the world was still pure, innocent, and unspoiled, work was part of God's blessings on mankind (see Genesis 2:15). It was one of the great pleasures that God gave to man when He formed him out of the dust of the earth because work gave man a purpose for his life. And that's why work will continue in heaven (see Revelation 22:3). God doesn't intend for us to float around on clouds all day while we play our little harps. Life will always have a purpose, and purpose will always demand work. So, our job as Christians is to work; God's job as Creator is to bless the work of our hands (see Deuteronomy 28:12) and to do those things that we cannot achieve through human effort. It's quite simple: If we will do the possible parts of life's equations (work), God will do the impossible parts of life's equations (prosperity). If we will do the natural parts (work), God will do the supernatural parts (success).

It is undeniable that God's promises of prosperity are contingent on our willingness to work, and perhaps that explains why the United States, in just two-and-a-half centuries, has become not just the wealthiest and most prosperous nation in the world, but the wealthiest and most prosperous nation in the *history* of the world. Our country was founded on Judeo-Christian ethics, and one of the most fundamental of those biblical ethics is the ethic of hard work. Unfortunately, that ethic is under attack today, and our nation feels the consequences. We are declining in both power and influence as a nation and the gap is rapidly closing in the economic advantages that we hold over other nations. One major reason for this rapid and steady decline is our decreasing commitment to the concept of hard work.

WHO'S IN CONTROL OF YOUR DESTINY?

In today's culture, there is a growing point of view that we are "owed" certain things. We are "owed" a living wage, we are "owed" health care, we are "owed" a place to live, and we are "owed" an outcome in life that is equal to our expectations and to everyone else's outcome. Some think it is the responsibility of everyone else—through the government—to make sure that we are comfortable, that we are safe, that we are healthy, and that we are well-fed and highly educated. But the Bible is clear: "If anyone will not work, neither shall he eat" (2 Thessalonians 3:10, NKJV). You don't have a right to life's most basic necessities; you have a right to earn those necessities for yourself and your family. (Take note, however, that the Bible is also clear that a godly society is responsible for taking care of those who cannot provide for themselves).

Be careful not to fall into the trap of thinking the way that the world thinks because the world has never respected God's way of thinking, and the world never will respect God's way of thinking. If you allow the godless nature of modern society to sway you, you will put as little effort as possible into your schooling, your work, and every other meaningful aspect of your life. You will look to others to take care of you and guarantee you a comfortable existence, and that approach will separate you from the blessings of God. The current culture is a spiritually rebellious culture, expressing their disdain for God in every way they know how. So, you can't allow the vacillating trends of thought that control the lives and destinies of unbelievers to influence you. The upside-down logic of a perishing world will always lead you away from the promises of God, not toward them.

> **IF YOU WANT TO SUCCEED IN LIFE, YOU NEED TO STEER CLEAR OF ALL THE SHORTCUTS TO PROSPERITY THAT THE WORLD WILL OFFER YOU.**

Here's something else the Bible boldly proclaims, something your father told you when you were younger: if you want to succeed in life, you need to steer clear of all the shortcuts to prosperity that the world will offer you. You need to steer clear of all the shortcuts to wealth, and you need to steer clear of all the "free" and "easy" stuff that society will make available to you because anything that's "free" can't be good. Not even salvation is free. Somebody had to die to pay for your sins.

Focus instead on the stakes that secure the tent of blessing. Focus on diligence. Focus on persistence. Focus on commitment, integrity, and the pursuit of a long-term vision for your life. Avoid all the "shortcuts" that are destined to lead you into poverty, and instead be diligent in your work (see Proverbs 10:4) because the person who is excellent in his work is the person who "will serve before kings" (Proverbs 22:29).

Our primary responsibility as Christians is to obey God's laws while learning to apply His principles to our daily lives. But while we work to do the things that glorify the Lord and position ourselves for His blessings, we also should do those things in order to demonstrate the power of God's Word to those who are observing our lives. God wants to bless us so we can be a blessing. More than likely, you read the Bible regularly, so you know from personal experience just how "on point" God's principles really are. But most of the people you encounter each day aren't people who are inclined to read the Bible. Instead, they are watching you and "reading" your life. They are taking note of your words and actions and comparing those words and actions to the things you claim to believe. So, in effect, you have become God's written word to them. You have become God's signpost in the wilderness. Most people around you won't give God the time of day, but those same people will notice you, especially if you tend to talk about your faith a lot, and your example will speak to them in a way that nothing else can. Your submission to the biblical laws of prosperity will point the people around you to God's paths of life and blessing in a way that no book or sermon ever could.

The Bible explains God's principles to us in some places but only allows us to see those principles at work in people's lives in other places. It is written this way because people tend to learn in different ways. Some people learn by hearing or by reading, and other people learn by seeing or by experiencing. So, the Bible "preaches" to us in some sections and then gives us examples from history or the natural world in other sections, and it is purposely constructed this way to help us better grasp the eternal principles that God wants us to believe, embrace, and apply to our lives.

For example, God uses the ant twice in the Bible as an illustration of helping people more fully grasp this biblical principle of a strong work ethic (see Proverbs 6:6; 30:25). The ant has no boss and no manager, yet it instinctively works to support itself and the other ants who depend on it. So, God directly teaches us about the principle of hard work using a tangible illustration from nature in the book of Proverbs to help us understand this same principle found elsewhere in the Bible. When we finally take action to apply that principle to our daily lives, He confirms the principle through the blessings He bestows on our lives. What a powerful behavioral modification strategy!

In the Bible, God also uses a lot of illustrations to help us understand the principle of hard work. While the ant serves as a constructive illustration of a godly work ethic, the lazy person serves as an antithetical example of this principle. While the ant prospers, the lazy person suffers, so God uses both illustrations to help us understand the different outcomes of these two opposing approaches to life (see Proverbs 6:9; 10:26; 13:4; 20:4). God teaches us from both the positive and negative sides of life because He wants us to understand that our choices are destined to produce consequences and that we need to take responsibility for the outcome of our own lives.

> **YOU DON'T HAVE TO ACCEPT POVERTY AS YOUR DESTINY.**

Nevertheless, as I have already explained, the poverty mindset is still the dominant mindset in the world today and, unfortunately, it is still the dominant mindset in large swaths of the church. The fatalistic approach to life is so common we can always expect poor people to surround us. (see Mark 14:7). The good news, however, is that you don't have to be one of those poor people. You don't have to accept poverty as your destiny. You can choose to stop violating God's principles and choose instead to embrace His ways so that you may prosper under God's favor and blessing, beginning with his oft-repeated principle of hard work.

It's one of the oldest lies out there, and people continue to fall for it every day—both as individuals and as a society—that it's possible to prosper while avoiding hard work. Instead, living off others; cheating, stealing, or lying to take advantage of other people; or participating in the latest get-rich-quick scheme is one way to prosper. But believing this lie is destined to lead to poverty and failure because you can't forever ignore the principles and the laws of God. Like the law of gravity, all the laws of God will eventually catch up to you. Eventually, gravity and all the rest of God's laws—including His law that laziness leads to catastrophe—will win, and you will face consequences.

I have to confess, though, that I see this terrible social trend toward work avoidance shifting back in the direction of sanity and sound judgment because our country seems to have tasted enough of the bitter fruits of our experimentation with spiritual rebellion in the marketplace, and now it appears that we are finally ready to reject the destructive approach to life that encourages us to depend on others, instead of ourselves, for happiness and fulfillment. Our country is gradually awakening to the fact that you can't pay people to do nothing (that's called "inflation") and that there is great reward in doing more than is required of you (that's called "going the extra mile"). As Christians and citizens of the most prosperous nation in human history, we should offer excellence in every aspect of our lives, especially in the aspects that pertain to our finances and labor. The Bible declares, "Whatever your hand finds to do, do it with all you might" (Ecclesiastes 9:10). "And whoever compels you to go one mile, go with him two" (Matthew 5:41, NKJV). These are the ways of the Lord, these were the ways of our fathers, these are the attitudes that stand in opposition to the mediocrity that pervades our present world, and these are the principles that will inevitably pay off with a prosperous lifestyle if we will choose to embrace them over the course of our lives.

But although there seems to be a shift taking place in our nation's attitude toward hard work and personal responsibility, the prevailing attitude in our country continues to be "something for nothing," and that attitude just won't work in the long run. As a nation, we can't expect to prosper if we continue to violate God's principles, and as individuals, we can't expect to prosper if we continue to reject God's ways. Politicians may try to convince us that we can get something for nothing, so they can garner a few votes in the next election, and certain leaders in our society may lie to us about the crippling effects of debt, so they can benefit from our undisciplined spending habits. But eventually, for those who violate the economic laws of God to pursue temporal pleasures or satisfy fleshly desires, the inevitable outcome will be poverty.

So, thank God that the tide is turning. Thank God that people are starting to awaken to the reality that sound economics are based on fixed laws that no one—including the government—can violate or ignore without consequence. Thank God that more and more people seem to be coming around to understanding the same economic laws that governed God's people in the past still serve as the proper path for us to walk in this present era, whether we are walking that path as individuals, as families, as churches, as businesses, or as a country.

WEALTH IS CREATED, NOT GUARANTEED

Are you a true believer? Are you looking to the Lord to bless you and to prosper you? Do you want to know what to do to position yourself for God's favor? No matter what kind of work you may do for a living, you need to pay close attention to your attitude toward that work. You need to become willing to put your very best efforts into your job and to work hard at it because when all is said and done, you're not actually working for a company. You're not even working for your boss or your client—you're really working for the Lord. You're working to honor God through the job He has given to you, so you can provide for yourself, your family, and your future and bear witness to Him through the excellence and integrity that you demonstrate as you engage your profession or your craft.

"But I don't really like my job that much," you might say. "This isn't what I want to do with my life."

Then make it easy for God to promote you. Prove yourself to be faithful and productive in the place where you work right now so that God can honor that attitude in your life by laying out a path for you that will lead to your ultimate destination. Remember, Joseph was Potiphar's slave and then assistant to the captain of the guard before he became the most powerful man in Egypt (next to Pharaoh). And for goodness' sake, be thankful. Be thankful for what you have right now so that God can trust you with more and more as you progress through life. You can't hate your job if you're thankful for your job, so learn to be thankful, and express your gratitude to the Lord every day through your words, your attitude, and your work ethic until He finally lifts you up to a higher place "in due season" (see Galatians 6:9).

The greatest things in life are those things that are done *through* us . . . not *by* us. So whatever God has placed in your hands to do, do it with all your might and do it to the best of your ability because, if you do, God will be glorified, and both God and man will notice, recognize, and promote you. Be the best architect you can be. Be the best doctor you can be. Be the best entrepreneur, mechanic, hairdresser, or stay-at-home mom that you can be because God always requires the best of us. In the Old Testament, He required the "best of the first fruits of your soil" (Exodus 23:19), and He still requires the best from us in everything we do. Besides, what we do in life and how well we do it reflects upon Him in a very big way. A person's work ethic and his attitude toward his work (and his employer) will probably testify more profoundly to his faith than any other testimony he could possibly contrive.

> **NOBODY EVER GOT RICH UNTIL SOMEBODY SHOWED A WILLINGNESS TO WORK HARD TO CREATE THAT WEALTH.**

Besides, in the end, all we really have in this life is time, and God has given all of us the same amount of it. Rich people don't have more time than poor people, and poor people don't have less time than rich people. It's what we choose to do with our time that makes the difference. There are twenty-four boxcars on your train to success every day, but the quality and the outcome of your life will boil down to what you put into those twenty-four boxcars. What you put into the precious hours of your life is what you will take out of them. So, make sure that you invest in the things that really matter, the things that can give you a meaningful return on your investment. Invest in the Lord, invest in your marriage and your family, invest in your church and the work of God, but also invest in yourself and your future by studying hard, working hard, and developing a godly work ethic that can bring you honor from God and man and pave the way to a life of blessing and prosperity. God never blesses *nothing*; He always blesses *something*. So become excellent at what you do, work hard at it, and put something in God's hands that He can bless because nobody ever got rich until somebody showed a willingness to work hard to create that wealth.

CHAPTER 8

GIVE AND PROSPER

Since the third day of creation, when God caused seed-bearing plants to burst forth from the elements of the ground, the divine law of sowing and reaping has existed, and it will continue to exist for as long as the earth remains. For "as long as the earth endures, seedtime and harvest, cold and heat, summer and winter, day and night will never cease" (Genesis 8:22). In fact, every area of God's creation and every principle of God's Word depend on this law because the law of sowing and reaping is the most fundamental law in God's creation and the basis for all His promises.

In the physical realms of life, we reap what we sow. In the spiritual realms of life, we reap what we sow (see Job 4:8; Hosea 10:12-13; Galatians 6:7-8). Before your salvation and mine could be procured, Jesus had to die and be buried so that his burial, like that of a seed, could produce a great harvest of redeemed souls (see John 12:23-24). Paul planted and Apollos watered to produce a harvest of souls in Corinth (see 1 Corinthians 3:6). And before your body can be raised to eternal life, it must be sown into the earth like a seed (see 1 Corinthians 15:42-22).

The law of sowing and reaping is something we can perceive in both the physical and spiritual realms of life. Likewise, it is relevant to the here and now, as well as eternity. But while we can perceive this established law of God's creation and while we can accept it as an eternal principle of both the physical and spiritual worlds, we will never understand precisely how it works. Nobody fully comprehends how a tiny seed can be buried in the cold, moist soil and then rise to produce a stalk of corn, a rapidly growing bamboo shoot, or a mighty oak. And yet it does! And the invisible seeds a person sows in the unseen aspects of his life are also guaranteed to produce a predetermined harvest because it is a fixed and irrevocable law of God's universe, a law that we must embrace and submit to, even though we have no clear understanding of how it works or why.

> **IF WE WANT TO REAP SOMETHING IN OUR LIVES, WE MUST SOW SOMETHING FIRST.**

Scientists have a basic understanding of how this law works when it comes to fruits and vegetables. They have a basic comprehension of how this law works when it comes to human and other biological life. But we humans, although capable of observing and recognizing this law at work in a lot of different aspects of creation, have no idea how it works in everyday life.

Some call it karma. Some call it "yin and yang." But regardless of what we call it, we need to recognize it as a reality, and we need to note that its origins lie in God and His creative Word because the principle is this: if we want to reap something in our lives, we must sow something first. We can't just wish for things and expect them to magically appear. We can't even pray for things and just expect them to materialize before our eyes. Before something can become a reality in life, we must plant something or sow something into the ground, into our lives, into our hearts, into our minds, or into our actions in the physical world. The type of seeds that we sow will determine the type of harvest we produce. That is the most basic law of God's creation and His eternal kingdom.

If you want more love from your husband or wife, you need to sow more "seeds" of love into your relationship with your husband or wife. If you want more respect from others, you need to sow more "seeds" of respect into your interactions with those people. If you want more friends, you need to put more effort into presenting yourself as friendly (see Proverbs 18:24). If you want more forgiveness, if you want more kindness, if you want more compassion, or if you just want more help moving your furniture into your new apartment, you need to sow those same "seeds" into the lives of others. If you do, you will "reap what you sow" and receive more of the same things you have invested in the lives of other people because everything that God has created is a type of "seed" that is specifically designed to produce more of itself... but not until it has been sown.

The principle works both ways: for good or for bad, for positive or for negative, for life or for death. If you sow good seeds, you will reap an abundant harvest of good returns, but if you sow bad seeds, you will reap the whirlwind (see Hosea 8:7) because the same ground that gives us beautiful tulips also gives us ugly and troublesome weeds. And that means that if you sow anger, you will reap anger from many of the people you encounter in life. If you sow criticism, you will be excessively and unfairly criticized. If you sow contention and quarreling, you will get a truckload of the same thing all the time, everywhere you go.

YOU REAP WHAT YOU SOW

Many of us have sown our "crops" for years without realizing it, and now the "fruits" we are reaping in our lives help us to easily identify the "seeds" we have been sowing. Jesus said, "By their fruits ye shall know them" (Matthew 7:16, ASV) because a piece of fruit bears witnesses to the type of "seeds" that gave it life, and the "fruit" in a person's life bears witness to the invisible "seeds" that person has been sowing into his or her marriage, children, work, relationships, and personal economics. The prophet Obadiah realized this when he wrote, "As you have done, it will be done to you; your deeds will return upon your own head" (Obadiah 1:15).

God's laws of sowing and reaping couldn't be any clearer. Both the Word of God and the repetitive testimony of daily life give credence to how a person must first *sow* whatever it is he wants *out* of his life. And while the seeds we sow can be *bad* seeds—which explains why we suffer from undesirable problems in our lives—the seeds we sow can also be *good* seeds. Sowing better seeds into our marriages will translate into better marriages, sowing better seeds into our interactions with others will translate into better relationships, and sowing better seeds into our walk with God will translate into a richer, deeper, and more powerful relationship with the Lord. All we must do is plant "seeds" that contain the same "genetic information" we want to multiply in our lives; then the seeds will do the rest by producing an inevitable harvest.

And it's no different with money. Money is not excluded from this universal and eternal principle. In those aspects of life that involve money and finance, just as in every other aspect of life, I reap what I sow. If I want to reap a harvest of financial blessing, I must sow some financial seeds, not seeds of love or forgiveness. In the physical world, I can't plant tomato seeds and pray that I get watermelons. It doesn't work that way. In the physical world, if I want watermelons, I have to plant watermelon seeds because the genetic code of the seed will determine what kind of harvest I reap. The spiritual world works the same way because God created both the spiritual and physical worlds. A person always receives a harvest that is based on the seeds that person has sown over the course of time. A person's life is primarily shaped in the physical realm, the spiritual realm, human relationships, and the economic realm and the type of seeds that person has sown into the visible and invisible dimensions of his or her life, including financial dimensions, will determine their outcomes.

Here's something I learned more than twenty years ago that I've applied to my life ever since. The principle is based on Ephesians 6:8 and has helped me frequently throughout my life: you don't always reap *where* you sow, but you do always reap *what* you sow.

> **YOU DON'T ALWAYS REAP WHERE YOU SOW, BUT YOU DO ALWAYS REAP WHAT YOU SOW.**

Paul told the Ephesians, "You know that the Lord will reward [you] for whatever good [you] do," and that is true. But while God never failed to reward Paul for all the good things he had done in his life, he didn't always reward Paul at the same moment he was doing those good things. Sometimes, God rewarded Paul later in life for things he had done earlier in his life, and God didn't fully reward Paul for his faithful life until Paul entered heaven (see 2 Timothy 4:7-8). With that thought in mind—that seeds of blessing don't always produce an immediate, overnight harvest—I decided that I would stop doing "favors" for people. Instead, I started "blessing" people and started looking to God to reward me later. The difference is significant because a favor is a loan. The recipient of a favor is indebted to the person who performed that favor for him, and that means that at some point in time, the person who performed the favor is going to expect the favor to be repaid (with interest). But when we sow a blessing into someone's life, instead of a favor, that person is no longer indebted to us. Instead, God is indebted to us, and God will always pay His debts at the right time and in the right way. In fact, He might even "postpone" some of those payments, so we can receive our rewards in heaven instead of here on earth, because God's rewards pay higher dividends the longer we leave those seeds in the ground so they can grow and mature (see Matthew 6:19-20).

Whenever I bless another person with my abilities, my time, my love, my kindness, or even my money, that gift represents a part of who I am. It's a "seed" that I sow into someone else's life, and because I am willing to invest it in another person's well-being, God will repay me for that act of service. Even if I offer something as simple as a cup of cold water, God will take notice and properly reward me at the right time for my selfless sacrifice (see Matthew 10:42).

In 2 Corinthians 9:8 (AMP), we learn:

God is able to make all grace [every favor and earthly blessing] come in abundance to you, so that you may always [under all circumstances, regardless of the need] have complete sufficiency in everything [being completely self-sufficient in Him], and have an abundance for every good work and act of charity.

God's blessings are tied directly to a person's attitude toward others, and a charitable attitude is a type of "seed" that a person can sow into other people's lives to produce a harvest of blessing in his own life.

But take note that this verse in 2 Corinthians does not tell us that God WILL make all grace come in abundance to us. Rather, this verse tells us that God is "ABLE to make all grace come in abundance to [us]." God's willingness to bless us depends on our willingness to sow seeds of personal sacrifice into the lives of others and into the work of His kingdom. As I have stated repeatedly, God never blesses *nothing*; He always blesses *something*. Our role in the miracle of divine blessing is to give God something that He can bless. Our role is to put something in God's hands that He can reward and multiply. We have to plant "seeds."

> **GOD WILL ONLY MULTIPLY THE SEEDS THAT WE SOW. HE WON'T MULTIPLY THE SEEDS THAT WE HOARD.**

Consequently, it doesn't matter what the world's economies may be doing right now because God is able, regardless of the circumstances, to make all grace abound in our lives. He is able to provide abundantly for us. All we must do is obey his law of sowing and reaping, so He will have a reason to bless us. Just think about it! This one little verse has more positive words (seven words in all, according to the KJV translation) than any other verse I can find in the Bible. This one little verse in the KJV uses the words *all, abound, always, all, all, abound,* and *every*. I don't know how God's Word could be any clearer. He can provide for us under any circumstances. But please, let me once again emphasize that this verse doesn't promise abundance to just anyone or everyone. It promises that God is "able" to pour out His measureless and abundant blessings on those who meet the preconditions set forth in the context of 2 Corinthians 9:6-8 which describes the "cheerful giver" who is willing to "sow generously" into the lives and the work of other people.

Because of the fixed, divine law of sowing and reaping, God will only multiply the seeds that we sow. He won't multiply the seeds that we hoard. He wants us to sow our seeds, not store them in a safe place or lock them inside a vault. Like the soil that awaits the farmer's seed, the hand of God will only multiply those seeds that we release to Him, not the ones that we grip tightly. The world tells me to hold onto my money and store it up for a future day of need, and there is a certain measure of wisdom in that sentiment. But while the return on investment for saved funds is limited, the return on investment for sown funds is virtually unlimited, especially in God's economy because planting—instead of preserving—is the only way that a seed of any type (agricultural or financial) can be multiplied. That's true in agriculture, that's true in the case of Jesus (who died and was buried so that He might become the firstborn among many brethren), and that's true in the financial arena.

The point here is that the law of sowing and reaping is both universal and eternal. It applies to physical things like agriculture, it applies to spiritual things like heavenly rewards, it applies to relational things like kindness, and it applies to our finances as well. But since this book is focused on the economic aspects of life and God's principles and laws concerning economics, I want to take this law of sowing and reaping and expound upon it from a strictly financial perspective. I want to address the subject of giving as a prerequisite for prosperity.

"Well, I'd like to give," you might say, "but I just don't have anything to give."

Not true! We all have something to give. It may be small, like the gift the widow who deposited just two small coins in the temple treasury (see Luke 21:1-4). But it's still a "seed" despite its limited value, and God has promised that He will bless us for sowing financial "seeds" into His kingdom. He has promised that He will bless, so we might have even more "seeds" to sow.

In fact, God has declared that He will always give seeds to the person who is willing to sow them (see 2 Corinthians 9:10), and He has made this promise because more seeds translate into more sowing as long as the sower doesn't succumb to the temptation of consuming too many of His seeds to feed his appetites. Of course, systematically setting aside a predetermined portion of those seeds, so we can sow them back into the soil of God's blessing, the same soil that gave us our seeds in the first place, is the best way to avoid the temptation to consume too many seeds. We can produce a reliable formula of divine blessing that will never, ever fail when we combine our faithfulness with God's provision of seeds.

All over the world, people are trying to reap a financial harvest without planting any financial seeds, and that is really perplexing to me because nobody in his right mind would go into his backyard to pick tomatoes unless he had previously planted some tomato seeds. Nevertheless, we somehow expect God to bless us financially when we have been unwilling to sow the necessary seeds into His work or into the lives or work of other people. You can't make withdrawals from your heavenly bank account if you've never made any deposits.

You make a living by what you get, but you make a life by what you give. I love to give. I live to give. Many people live beyond their means, but my goal is to give beyond my means! What are you giving? Do you live a life of giving?

My question to you at this point is: Do you have any financial problems or great financial needs? My second question is: What kind of financial seeds have you been sowing that could produce a harvest sufficient to meet your current needs? My third question is: Did you sow those seeds sparingly or bountifully, and did you sow them begrudgingly or with a cheerful heart (see Proverbs 11:24; 2 Corinthians 9:7)?

We all know that we just can't out-give God. But do we REALLY believe it? Here's the amazing part about giving. We are told to give; the Bible is clear on this. And yet, when we obey the command to give, we are then rewarded. It's a beautiful cycle of giving and blessing, sowing and reaping, which leads to more generosity and an overflow of abundance!

There are three "gives" to remember:

1) Give as it has been given to you. Paul reminds us in Romans 8:32 that God "did not spare his own Son, but gave him up for us all—how will he not also, along with him, graciously give us all things?" We have been blessed beyond measure, so our response is to give and bless others.

2) Give now! Don't hesitate. Don't sit there and wonder, "Does God want me to give?" Of course He does. Giving is like voting—do it early and often!! Do it before you're asked to give. Make it a habit and give often.

3) Give to the degree you want to be blessed. If you want God to bless you just a little, give just a little. If you want him to "open the windows of heaven" on you, give with that same abandon. It is impossible to out-give God, but you must

provide a pathway for Him to give back to you, and the means of financial blessing that God has established as a law in His kingdom is the means of sowing and reaping. In agriculture and finance, God can give us WHAT we sow and MORE THAN we sow, but not until AFTER we sow. There is no mechanism for getting around this formula.

Yet God doesn't just bless us directly whenever we sow seeds into His work; He also blesses us indirectly. He doesn't just open the windows of heaven and pour out blessings that we are unable to contain; He also seals all the leaks in our barrels, so the rain from heaven isn't wasted and doesn't "leak" out of our lives. That's what God means when He says, "I will rebuke the devourer for your sakes" (Malachi 3:11, KJV).

It's nice to be the recipient of God's divine favor, and it's nice to see the windows of heaven opened over our lives so that God's financial blessings can be poured upon us. Yet that is the type of consistent blessing that I can expect when I willingly, joyfully, and liberally sow my financial seeds into God's work and the advancement of His kingdom. But what good is all that favor from above if the "barrel" that holds all those blessings is riddled with "leaks" and the spigot is wide open, causing all the "rain" from above to spill out onto the ground?

Obviously, if I'm going to live a blessed life, I will need God to open the windows of heaven and pour out His blessings from above, and He has promised to do that if I will faithfully sow into His kingdom. But if countless "holes" and "leaks" in the "barrel" that capture those same blessings are being constantly depleted, then God's financial favor will prove meaningless. If God's blessings of prosperity are being endlessly depleted through breakage, decay, rot, theft, or any other type of deterioration or robbery, then those blessings are being wasted, and they will do me no good.

That's why God promises not only to "open for you the windows of heaven," but also to "rebuke the devourer for your sakes" (Malachi 3:10-11, NKJV). Both types of blessing are needed if God intends for us to prosper, and we can see an excellent illustration of this in the history of the Jewish people. When the Jews were roaming the wilderness for forty years under the guidance of Moses, they were generous people. They weren't always obedient to the Lord, and they often incited God's wrath, but they were never accused of being stingy with their resources. The resources that the Egyptians handed over to them when they were preparing to flee from Egypt (see Exodus 12:36) are the same resources that the Israelites willingly sowed into God's work so that the tabernacle could be constructed according to the directions that God had given to Moses (see Exodus 35:20-29). So, the Hebrew people, despite their many flaws and inconsistencies, were generous people who were faithful in their giving. For that reason, God poured down manna from heaven (see Exodus 16:1-36), and extended the life of their clothing and their shoes (see Deuteronomy 29:5). He opened the windows of heaven to provide for their needs, but He also rebuked the devourer down below to minimize the rot, the decay, and the decomposition of the things He had provided for them.

He won't just bless us, but He will prevent the enemy from taking what is ours. He will rebuke the devourer. For example, when I bought a house in Florida, the inspectors told us the air conditioning units only had one year left on them, so I knew we would have to keep an eye on them. I didn't want to have to replace them, and to everyone's surprise, they lasted ten more years! See, He will cause things that should normally rot or decay to live. He will rebuke the devourer. The air conditioning units right now at our church are thirty years old. They should have given out years ago ... but God!

Those are just two simple examples, but I know this to be true, time and time again: God will rebuke the devourer for our sakes when we are faithful in our giving. He will rebuke theft. He will rebuke decay. He will rebuke mold, mildew, rot, breakage, and spoilage. That's not to say that your car and your shoes will last forever. All our "stuff" is destined to succumb to the physical elements, but the roof on your house and the tires on your car will last a lot longer when God rebukes the devourer because you have been faithful to sow your financial seeds into His kingdom.

THE FOUNDATION OF A PROSPEROUS LIFE

The principle of giving isn't confined to individuals. It's also a corporate responsibility. God's requirements for giving (as prerequisites for His blessings) certainly have an individual application, but we sometimes fail to realize that these requirements also apply to us collectively as churches. A giving church—a church that sows into the work of God both locally and globally—is a church that is vibrant and thriving. It is a church that will grow in its attendance as it grows in its charity because the more that people participate in God's economic plan for advancing His work, the healthier that body of believers will be. Tithing and growth go hand in hand, both for individual believers, businesses, and for churches.

God gives each person enough resources so that that person will have some "seeds" to sow into God's kingdom, and God gives each church enough resources so that that church will have some "seeds" to sow into God's kingdom. But to reap the benefits of God's blessings (showers of blessing from above and the rebuke of the devourer's efforts to consume those blessings here below), each individual and each church will need to do its part to remain faithful to the Lord. Like the Israelites in the wilderness, all of us will need to do our part in sowing seeds into God's kingdom so that churches won't have to rely on fundraisers and bake sales or other pitiful substitutes for faithful giving to survive. If everyone in our churches would tithe 10 percent of their income, the church would have no financial needs. If we will be faithful to sow the seeds that God has placed in our hands, all of us, including our churches, will be blessed with so many financial resources there won't be enough room to receive them.

So, the principle of sowing and reaping works for individuals. It also works for families and churches. But I would go one step further and say that this same principle works for businesses and even countries because the blessings that God bestows on various nations are based on the same criteria He uses to bless individuals and ministries. Perhaps this explains why the United States, despite its many flaws, has been blessed more abundantly than any nation in human history. From our inception, we have always been a generous nation (helping other nations) and a generous people (helping other people), and God has honored us by blessing us accordingly.

    I believe that churches should boldly proclaim the principle of giving. I believe that churches should embrace it and practice it themselves, but I also believe that churches should teach it to their constituents so that their constituents can practice this principle in their own lives, and I believe that parents should teach it to their children because this principle—the principle of practicing the law of sowing into God's kingdom in trust and reaping His promised blessings—is the foundation of a prosperous life. After all, my parents taught me this very principle when I was a young child, and I have believed it and practiced it throughout my entire life. As a result, God's blessings have always followed me, especially as I have come to more fully understand how this principle should be manifested in my daily life.

CHAPTER 9

ESTABLISH YOUR TRUE MOTIVES

We have discussed the principle of tithing, and we have discussed the connection that exists between a person's giving and God's blessings. The tithe (the first tenth of a person's increase) belongs to the Lord, but God's blessings are dramatically increased in a person's life as that person learns to present offerings to the Lord that are representative of His growing prosperity and above and beyond His tithe.

We have also discussed the principle of sowing and reaping, and we have examined that it is impossible to reap any type of harvest (agricultural, financial, or spiritual) unless we first sow the appropriate types of "seeds" and allow those "seeds" to take root and grow until they produce a harvest in our lives. We have analyzed the biblical concept of sacrifice and the connection that exists between our willingness to give and God's willingness to open the windows of heaven over our lives.

While all these concepts of stewardship are important, the motivations that drive them are equally important. God is always interested in *what* we do. He is always interested in the decisions we make and the actions we take, as well as the actions we choose not to take. But God is just as interested in the motivations that drive those actions as He is in the actions themselves because while man is prone to look at the external factors of a person's life, God looks at the heart (see 1 Samuel 16:7). So, to the Lord, it's not just about the things we do; it's also about the thinking and the hidden desires that give birth to the things we do.

With that in mind, I want to devote this chapter to the exploration of three motives that need to accompany our giving. God will bless us whenever we give, regardless of the motives that may drive us because that is the irrevocable law of sowing and reaping that dominates His creation. If we are willing to sow the necessary seeds, He will reward us with a harvest, regardless of what may motivate us to make that sacrifice. However, just because we have sown seeds and reaped a harvest doesn't mean that God is pleased with our actions, and it doesn't mean that He will fully prosper us. God is intensely interested in *why* we have sown those seeds and what we intend to do with the harvest that they yield. In other words, God is interested in the motives that compel us to give.

THE MOTIVE OF FAITHFULNESS

The first motivation that should drive our giving, the type of giving that is pleasing to God, is the motivation of faithfulness. One of my favorite parables in the Bible is the parable of the talents and the three servants. The master (Jesus) was preparing to take a long trip. In anticipation of his departure, the master gave talents ("bags of gold" in the NIV translation) to his three servants. To the first servant, he gave five talents, to the second servant, he gave two talents, and to the third servant, he gave one talent because each servant had demonstrated a different level of competence in managing his master's affairs. Then, the master left on his journey without giving his servants any specific instructions regarding how they should handle their master's money. You can read the complete parable in Matthew 25:14-30.

Sometime later, the master returned from his trip, and he called his three servants to account. I think you know the rest of the story. The first servant had invested the five talents that were entrusted to him, so he returned ten talents to his master. He had doubled his master's resources. The second servant had invested the two talents that were entrusted to him, so he returned four talents to his master, also doubling the resources that had been placed in his care. But the third servant did nothing with his single talent (or bag of gold). He just hid it away for safekeeping and returned it to his master when his master came back from his journey.

The third servant, who had failed to properly handle his master's money, was rebuked and severely punished, which tells us that God expects us to use our gifts and talents (including the finances He has entrusted to us) to advance His kingdom. He doesn't just want us to "sit" on those things or to "tread water." But the two servants who had properly "sown" their master's resources were praised and richly rewarded because they had done a good thing. They had sown the "seeds" that the master had placed in their hands, and they had produced something with those "seeds" that brought increase to their master. Consequently, they were lauded as "good and faithful" servants, and they were invited to share in their master's bounty.

The key word here is *faithful*. They accepted their responsibility to faithfully protect their master's resources. They accepted their responsibility to faithfully "sow" or "invest" their master's wealth. They accepted their responsibility to faithfully return the master's talents to him with interest at the appropriate time. They protected their master's resources, but they did more than that. They also multiplied their master's resources, and that is the attitude that the master wanted to see in his servants. It is the attitude that elicited both his praise and his rewards.

When you die and go to heaven, the sweetest words you could ever hope to hear are the words, "Well done, good and faithful servant" (Matthew 25:23). God has entrusted you with many "talents." He has entrusted you with many gifts, with education, with knowledge, and with accumulated wisdom. He has entrusted you with experience, training, professional connections, and an array of additional benefits and resources that you use every day to sustain yourself and advance your own agendas. But God also wants you—indeed, He expects you—to use those same resources, especially your financial resources, to help build and advance His kingdom. He wants and expects you to "invest" all these things in the work of His kingdom, and your faithfulness (or lack thereof) will be key to how reliably you fulfill your responsibility as a "servant" of the Lord. It will be key to whether you hear those precious words of praise and recognition when you finally stand before the throne of God.

> **WHETHER YOUR TITHE IS LARGE OR SMALL, GOD IS ALWAYS INTERESTED IN HOW FAITHFULLY YOU GIVE IT.**

Don't just give occasionally; give regularly and systematically. Don't just give when you feel like it; give when you don't feel like it. Don't just give when your coffers are full; give when your coffers are running low. Don't just give when you go to church; give on those weekends when you can't attend church. Be faithful in your giving. Take it seriously. Regard it as a holy responsibility. Always be able to look at yourself in the mirror and say, "I have removed the sacred *portion* from *my* house, and have also given it" (Deuteronomy 26:13, NASB).

God is not that interested in the size of your gift. The widow in Luke 21:1-4 gave very little because she possessed very little, so the size of your gift should be proportional to your personal earnings. But whether your tithe is large or small, God is always interested in how faithfully you give it. Faithfulness is one of those traits that God will richly reward both in this world and the world to come.

THE MOTIVE OF LOVE

The second motivation that should stir our giving is the motivation of love. Without love, all our giving—in fact, everything we do in life—is in vain because God is love, and everything He does is motivated by love, so only human actions driven by love can please Him.

In his first letter to the Believers in Corinth, Paul wrote extensively about love, and he summarized love's connection to giving by saying, "If I give everything I own . . . but I don't love, I've gotten nowhere" (1 Corinthians 13:3, MSG). So, it's not just about the numbers. It's not just about moving the decimal point one place to the left to calculate a tenth of your increase, so you can write a check and fulfill your financial obligations to the Lord. God is more interested in your heart and the motivation for your giving than He is in your rote repetition of dropping a check in the offering plate.

Some people understand the first motivation that drives real giving. Some people give faithfully, systematically, and regularly. They compute their tithes with the same diligence that the Pharisees employed when they counted out a tenth of the leaves from the mint and the cumin plants that grew in their gardens (see Matthew 23:23). And God will bless these people for their faithfulness. But unless love motivates a person's giving so that his faithful giving becomes more than just a respectable discipline, that giving will have an aspect of emptiness about it that will never allow the giver to enjoy true fulfillment or the kind of divine blessing that can lead to lasting prosperity.

As early as the fourth chapter of Genesis, we find people worshiping God by bringing their offerings to Him. Cain and Abel were both faithful. Both worshiped the Lord regularly by preparing offerings that consisted of the first fruits from the soil and the firstborn of their flocks and herds. But while God looked upon Abel's offering with favor, He viewed Cain's offering with disdain, not because Cain's offering was inferior in any way and not because Cain had been unfaithful or irregular in his giving but because Cain's motivation for giving was apparently less than what God expected. Abel was a righteous man (see Matthew 23:35) while Cain's heart was infected with impure motivations and bitterness (see Genesis 4:6). God wants us to know that giving—the kind of giving that produces divine favor in our lives and results in real and perpetual prosperity—is more than just an act of self-discipline; it is also an act of love. A love for God, a love for God's kingdom, and a love for God's people are necessary if we want to present acceptable sacrifices to the Lord that He can bless in tremendous ways. Why? Because God is more interested in the heart than He is in formalities. He is more interested in the higher law of love than He is in the ritualistic practice of writing a check. Only love alone has real or eternal value, and only love alone can open the channels through which God can richly bless our lives.

Few verses in the Bible are quoted more frequently than Luke 6:38 (NKJV), where Jesus said,

> *"Give, and it will be given to you: good measure, pressed down, shaken together, and running over will be put*

into your bosom. For with the same measure that you use, it will be measured back to you."

In other words, if we give, we can expect to receive back from the Lord, and we can expect to receive in proportion to our giving because as I have already explained in detail, we are sowing "seeds" into God's kingdom, and those "seeds" are designed to produce an abundant harvest in our lives. Giving, therefore, should be a natural act in the same way that breathing is a natural act. But unlike breathing, we must pay attention to *why* we give as much as we pay attention to *when* we give or *how much* we give because the Bible stresses the importance of motivation in our giving as much as it stresses the importance of faithfulness. Paul implores us to give cheerfully (see 2 Corinthians 9:7), generously (see 2 Corinthians 9:6), and with a motivation of love (see 1 Corinthians 13:3).

> **THE KIND OF LOVE THAT IS DESCRIBED IN THE BIBLE IS A LOVE EXPRESSED THROUGH ACTIONS, NOT FEELINGS.**

Some people consider love to be an emotion, but in the Bible, love is not really regarded as an emotional aspect of life. When we think of love, we think of romance, we think of Valentine's Day, and we think of a deep emotional attachment to another person. But the biblical concept of love is quite different. The biblical concept of love is always attached to actions, not feelings. When Jesus said, "Love your enemies" (Matthew 5:44), He was not telling the people in the crowd that day to have warm, fuzzy feelings toward those who hated them. The people who heard Jesus's words that day understood what He was saying: they were to perform kind acts of service for those who hated them. The kind of love that is described in the Bible is a love expressed through actions, not feelings. Feelings have absolutely nothing to do with it.

When we consider God's love for us, we can better understand the Bible's concept of love. God expresses His love for us primarily through the things He does for us, not through heartfelt emotions or affectionate words. He forgives our sins, He comforts us in times of distress, He restores the souls of those who have been broken by the challenges and hardships of life, and He died on a cross to hide our sins from his own righteous wrath. In the Greek language, therefore, the word *love* is an action word, not a conceptual word. It speaks to positive actions toward others, not warm feelings toward others.

So, giving is an expression of love toward God because giving is an action, not a feeling or a sentiment. "For God so loved the world that he GAVE" (John 3:16, NKJV, emphasis added). And that's the point: if God gives to us to demonstrate His love for us, then we should give to Him to demonstrate our love for Him. Consequently, if you truly love the Lord, you will want to give to Him, just as you enjoy giving to others you love . . . and you will want to give to Him in every imaginable way. You will want to give Him your time and your attention, you will want to give Him your praise, you will want to offer Him your unique talents, and you will want to give Him a meaningful portion of the resources with which He has blessed you. Real love will compel you to give to God the same way it compels you to give to your spouse, your children, and all the other people in your life who fill your heart and occupy your thoughts.

Besides, money is the most ideal tangible representation of our lives, so it is the most fitting gift to give to God. Every dollar we hold in our hands is a tangible representation of a portion of the most precious aspects of our lives, and that is why it is the best gift we could possibly offer to the Lord. And why is that?

That dollar bill in your wallet is nothing more and nothing less than a physical representation of a portion of your talents because you had to share some of your talents with someone else to earn that dollar bill. Likewise, that dollar bill represents a portion of your time (which is irreplaceable) because you had to sacrifice some of your time in exchange for that dollar bill. And that dollar bill represents a portion of the effort you had to put forth to learn your trade, hone your professional skills, or accumulate the wisdom and experience that other people would need and for which they would be willing to pay you. So, to surrender that dollar bill to God is to surrender a portion of your time, your talents, and all the other precious and irreplaceable parts of your life to Him. And that's what makes it such a suitable gift. That's what makes it the most meaningful and precious sacrifice you could possibly offer to the Lord because you're not just giving God a piece of paper money. You are giving Him a portion of your life. You are giving Him the time and effort that you spent learning your trade and practicing your craft. You are giving Him all the effort and hard work you had to put into earning that piece of currency. It is for these reasons that money is the best gift you could possibly offer to the Lord, especially when it becomes a "pleasing aroma" to Him because you are offering it with the right motives and for all the right reasons (see Leviticus 3:5).

> **WHETHER THAT PERSON RECOGNIZES IT OR NOT, GOD IS THE ONE WHO MADE IT POSSIBLE FOR HIM TO SUCCEED.**

The sacrifice of a dollar bill represents the sacrifice of your gifts, your talents, your experiences, your abilities, your time, and your energy to the Lord. It also represents a sacrifice of your personal needs and wants because you deprive yourself of a treasure or an experience that you could purchase with that dollar bill when you give that dollar bill to God instead. You place Him above yourself when you surrender a portion of your hard-earned cash to God on a regular basis. You prioritize His agenda above your own, and that is a worthy and noble expression of your love. When given in that spirit, rather than a spirit of compulsion or obligation, the offering of your finances is absolutely one of the best ways you can give yourself to God.

I know that a lot of people might disagree with me, but I am convinced that there is no such thing as a self-made millionaire or billionaire because regardless of how a person makes his money, all that knowledge, all that experience, and all those professional connections originated with God. Whether that person recognizes it or not, God is the one who made it possible for him to succeed, and that is why work is so important to the Lord. That is why God encourages all believers to find meaningful employment and to work diligently with their hands (see 2 Thessalonians 3:10; Proverbs 10:4). Work is a means of earning money, which can then be sown into God's kingdom and the lives of God's people (see Ephesians 4:28). If we don't work, we won't have the money we need to live. If we don't work, we also won't have the money to give so that God can bless us. Money is what we have when we turn our time, talents, gifts, experiences, energy, loyalties, and abilities into tangible assets that we can actively and deliberately place in the rich soil of God's kingdom, reap a bountiful return, and experience the Lord's blessings in our lives.

> **GOD PUT US ON THIS EARTH, NOT TO SEE HOW MUCH WE COULD GATHER, BUT TO SEE HOW MUCH OF HIS LOVE WE MIGHT SPREAD TO OTHERS.**

Jesus summarized the essence and the purpose of life in nine simple words: "It is more blessed to give than to receive" (Acts 20:35). So, the question becomes: do you really believe what Jesus said when He uttered those words, or do you secretly believe that the primary purpose of life is to look out for yourself? God put us on this earth, not to see how much we could gather, but to see how much of His love we might spread to others. He put us on this earth to see how much love we might show him by our willingness to elevate His eternal purposes above our own temporary ones. That is why a person's mindset about giving is just as important or perhaps more important than the amount of money he gives. That is why a person's motivation for giving is just as important or perhaps more important than the size of the check he brings to church on Sunday. That is why love must be the primary driving motivation behind our giving because only love can compel us to make the kinds of personal sacrifices that God requires from His faithful servants. In the end, it won't be about how much you received. In the end, it is how much you gave that will define your life. How much time, how much attention, how much help, how much wisdom, how much support, how much encouragement, and how many resources God could use to bless others!

Let's face it! Jesus could have fed those five thousand people without the aid of those five fish and two loaves of bread. But Jesus waited for that young boy to offer his meager meal to Him, then the Lord blessed that small offering, multiplied it, and used it to enrich the lives of thousands of people. And so, it is with you and with me! God doesn't need us to convert the nations. He doesn't need us to deliver those who are captive to various addictions. He doesn't need us to build His church or to spread the gospel. But for some reason that is beyond my understanding, He waits for us to present our seemingly insignificant offerings to Him, and then He multiplies those offerings and uses them to do great and mighty things in the world. He uses them because He knows they were presented to Him as expressions of our love.

THE MOTIVE OF GENEROSITY

The final motivation for giving is generosity. Some people just have a generous nature, and some people don't, but I have noticed over the past few years that the concept of generosity seems to be growing dimmer by the day in our nation.

Over the past several generations, the United States has shown itself to be the most generous nation on earth. Through our churches, we have supported world evangelization at a level that no other nation can rival. Through our global business ventures, we have helped lift more of the world's people out of poverty than any nation before us. Through our federal government, we have been the world's leading contributor to international efforts combatting illiteracy, disease, infant mortality, and malnutrition. I believe that the United States is the wealthiest nation in the history of mankind because God has blessed our nation for its generous attitude toward others. Even within our own borders, the citizens of the United States have shown themselves to be the world's most liberal givers to charitable efforts designed to help hurting people.

But today, our nation is in decline, and our economy is in decline as well. I believe that this decline is at least partly related to the regression of generosity we are witnessing within our country. I believe that life becomes progressively purposeless and increasingly less meaningful whenever we start focusing all our time, attention, and resources on ourselves. On the other hand, I believe that life becomes more purposeful and increasingly fulfilling as we turn our attention outward to a hurting world with a conscious awareness of the needs of other people. Even those who profess no faith in God have, on many occasions, come to acknowledge that a life defined by an outward vision is a life of greater satisfaction.

> **FROM GOD'S PERSPECTIVE, IT'S NOT ABOUT HOW MUCH LOVE YOU CAN GET BUT HOW MUCH LOVE YOU CAN GIVE.**

But this concept of generosity is even more relevant for the believer because God's favor depends in large measure upon our willingness to be generous toward others. God wants all of us who confess our faith in Him to experience the deep, internal satisfaction that can only come from a lifestyle of generosity, self-sacrifice, and an outward gaze toward a world in need.

From God's perspective, it's not about how much love you can get but how much love you can give. It's not about how much encouragement you need but how much encouragement you can offer to others. And it's not about how much money you can accumulate for yourself but how much money you can give to bless others and expand God's work in the world. Untold millions of people have this formula backward. They believe it's about them. But God's greatest desire for each of us is that we might learn to focus on the needs of the people around us so that God can take care of our needs.

Like you, I don't like to think about the inevitability of my own death, but when I do think about it, I know that I want to die broke and exhausted. I want to give it all, and I want to leave it all on the table because I know that "it is more blessed to give than to receive" (Acts 20:35). Why? For four reasons: First, when I give freely and generously, I put God first in my life. I put the Lord ahead of my own selfish desires, and my obedience to His commands puts me in a position where He is more willing and likely to bless me.

Second, I demonstrate my trust in Him when I liberally give to God and to the needs He places before me. I boldly proclaim that I am confronting my own natural and human fear of lack and trust Him to honor His Word in my life when I give to Him and others in His name. I don't fully understand why, but I know that nothing commands the attention of God, and nothing moves Him more powerfully than a willingness to trust Him. The Bible is full of examples where God literally parted the waters, raised the dead, or stopped the earth from rotating on its axis because a mere mortal like you and me was willing to trust Him. When I trust the Lord with my future and with my very survival by surrendering to Him a portion of my hard-earned income, that demonstration of faith profoundly touches and "moves" Him to do great things in my life.

> **GENEROSITY IS GOD'S "PREVENTIVE MEDICINE" FOR SPIRITUALLY DEADLY DISEASES LIKE SELFISHNESS, GREED, COVETOUSNESS, AND A ME-FIRST MINDSET AND LIFESTYLE.**

Third, giving generously to the Lord protects me from the moral decay associated with greed. God is more interested in my heart than any other part of my life. He is more interested in the state of my heart than any temporary problem that I may face because the condition of my heart has eternal ramifications, while my earthly problems are temporary and will often work themselves out. So, generosity is God's "preventive medicine" for spiritually deadly diseases like selfishness, greed, covetousness, and a me-first mindset and lifestyle.

Finally, when I learn to give freely and generously, God will trust me with greater resources. Remember, when the master returned from his journey to confront the three servants he had entrusted with his wealth, two of those servants proved to be worthy of his future trust while the third proved to be unworthy. But notice what the master did when he confronted the unworthy servant. The master rebuked that unfaithful servant and punished him, and then the master took that servant's talent and gave it to the servant who had shown himself to be the most reliable in managing his master's resources.

God will entrust you with blessings that are directly proportional to the faithfulness you have demonstrated with His past blessings. The more faithful you prove yourself to be, the more blessings He will entrust to you. He will not perpetually bless those who have proven themselves unworthy of His blessings. Instead, He will "redirect" those resources to those who have shown themselves to be in alignment with His plan to build churches, to change lives, and to meet the needs of hurting people.

Truly, it is more blessed to give than to receive. It is more blessed for us, and it is more blessed for others when we become willing to give to the Lord. But remember, it's not just about the act of giving. It's not just about how much we give or how often. It's also about *why* we give because "People look at the outward appearance, but the LORD looks at the heart" (1 Samuel 16:7).

Learn to give cheerfully, not grudgingly or out of necessity (see 2 Corinthians 9:7). In other words, make your giving an act of worship and an act of celebration. Make it an occasion when you can reflect with gratitude upon all the blessings and opportunities that God has bestowed upon you. The Greek translation for *cheerfully* in this verse means "hilariously, noisily, and with fun and laughter." And as strange as it may seem to some believers, that is exactly the attitude God wants us to display whenever we give to Him. He wants us to give because we are grateful. He wants us to give because we recognize Him as the source of all our provision. He wants us to give and to give faithfully because we love Him and have elevated Him to the utmost position in our hearts and lives. He is never pleased whenever we give "grudgingly." In other words, He is never pleased when we give solely out of obligation or necessity because we fear what others might think of us if we don't.

Giving should be a celebration. It should be a celebration of God's past faithfulness, and it should be a celebration of our present contentment and faith-driven expectation for increased blessings in the future. We should be happy because we know that God is going to see our gifts and give them back to us with interest. We should be happy because we know that faithful giving driven by love and gratitude will build the church, feed people, teach children, and spread the gospel to others. Lives will be changed.

CONCLUSION

ON EARTH AS IT IS IN HEAVEN

As I mentioned in my introduction, my primary objective for this book was to list and explain some of the most basic laws of economics that God has laid down for us in the pages of the Bible. I wanted to clearly establish how God is the originator of wealth and the author of all genuine prosperity, and that His many promises regarding the well-being of His saints are conditioned upon their understanding of and obedience to the fixed laws of finance that He has established for both heaven and earth.

I sincerely hope that one of your key takeaways from this book is that God's laws of economics are not "mysterious." They are not hidden "gems" of revelation that those persistent enough to dig them out from the text will mine and discover. Rather, they are clearly enunciated and clearly explained. In fact, the writers of Scripture frequently repeat these laws in different contexts so that any reader can find them, understand them, remember them, and learn to apply them to his or her life.

As I wrap up my thoughts regarding God's laws of economics, I want to emphasize that these laws are primarily intended for earthly life, not heavenly life. Yes, all of God's financial laws apply to heaven because they are fixed and eternal. But they also apply to life here on earth. And when you think about it, God's laws of economics apply more to earthly life than to heavenly life because, once we get to heaven, we're not going to have to think about these laws or submit to them. Instead, they will be universally understood and universally applied, and every person in heaven will live in God's abundance. So, all the financial principles explained to us in the Bible are more relevant to us while we are here on earth than they will be throughout the vast ages of eternity.

Yet despite their central role in a prosperous earthly life, many people, just don't believe in the promises of God or the fixed economic laws of God's Word, and they don't accept God's principles for financial success. They reject these biblical concepts because they believe that God's promises of blessing just don't apply to them and don't work for them. However, as Solomon said to the Israelites at the dedication of the temple in Jerusalem, "Not one word has failed of all the good promises God has made to us" (Joshua 21:45, author paraphrase). God's promises and the principles of God's Word will stand, and those Christians who struggle in this modern world will have to decide whether they will believe these principles and promises or yield to the conventional wisdom of a lost and hopeless world. They will have to decide whether they will listen to the voices of the many authors of Scripture and the many millions of faithful believers who have experienced God's faithfulness for themselves or allow unbelieving people who have never even studied God's economic laws and who certainly have never submitted to or practiced those laws to shape their thinking.

I have personally spent hundreds, perhaps thousands of hours studying the principles I have shared with you in this book, and, as you already know, I have spent more than twenty-five years practicing the things I have learned. From that position of authority, I boldly submit to you to not allow people who have never even read most of God's promises regarding prosperity to discourage you. A person with an experience is never at the mercy of a person with an opinion, so trust my research and life experiences, and trust the testimony of great men like Paul, John, and Solomon. All the promises of God regarding prosperity and all the laws of God regarding the principle of sowing and reaping are as reliable as the morning sunrise. Therefore, as you read these promises and think about them day after day and year after year, as you practice them and learn to make them a fixture in your life, understand that God's truths will increasingly "renew" your mind, and your behaviors will change. Every righteous endeavor you put your hand to will pave a new direction for your life and bestow you with greater blessings.

I wrote this book because I want to see you prosper as God desires for you to prosper. I believe that God wants His people to walk through the fire without being burned (see Isaiah 43:2). I believe that when all the principles of worldly economics finally start to fail due to the nations' collective rebellion against God and collective abandonment of His ways, He wants to position His people to "do well" in those difficult times and move forward financially, rather than backward. Remember, when the seven-year famine came to Egypt, Joseph had a plan that allowed the Egyptian people and his own family to prosper during those years of turmoil. In the same way, God has a plan that will enable you to prosper while the rest of the world is struggling. After all, in every "season" of economic crisis, there are always some people who "win" and who come out ahead. Why shouldn't you be one of those people?

But there's one more reason I have written this book: the people of God need to continue their forward thrust in fulfilling the Great Commission. The church has grown significantly over the past several generations, but we still have a lot of work to do to "go into all the world and preach the gospel to every creature" (Mark 16:15, NKJV), and we will need a lot of resources to finish this work.

The Great Commission isn't just for pastors and missionaries. It's the responsibility of every believer; so, all believers need to work together to take the gospel to "all the nations" (Matthew 24:14; 28:19, NKJV). I believe God wants us to build His kingdom and use our prosperity to do just that! No matter what our economy may look like, we don't have faith in worldly sources of income, but our economic strategy is directly linked to God's Word. Some will serve on the frontlines as evangelists, church planters, and cross-cultural missionaries. Others will remain in their homelands, so they can provide the resources that the frontline workers will need. But in the end, every Christian will need to share in the responsibility of spreading the gospel throughout his or her community and into every nation and culture on the face of the earth because God's command to build His kingdom and to sow the seeds of His Word in people's hearts must become our highest priority.

As you embrace the Scriptures I have shared and as you think about and meditate on them day after day, may your mind be renewed, may you come to increasingly grasp the superiority of God's ways over the world's ways, and may you never stop receiving new revelations as you read these Scriptures, memorize them, confess them, and apply them to your everyday life and personal decisions, including your financial ones. May you create your own economy that is based upon God's model of prosperous living. And regardless of the circumstances that may surround you or the times in which you may be forced to live, may you always be fully prepared for the inevitable storms of life and the providential opportunities that God will place in your path. If you will walk in His ways, you will never fail to have enough to live and enough to give, and you will victoriously navigate all the seasons of your life and all the manmade economic disasters that may arise as God prepares the world for the return of His Son. And the rest of your life WILL be the best of your life.

> **THE REST OF YOUR LIFE, WILL BE THE BEST OF YOUR LIFE!**

CONNECT WITH DR. DAVE!

📷 @drdavemartin

🐦 @drdavemartin

in /davemartininternational

▶ /thedrdavemartin

f /drdavemartin

CHANGE YOUR MIND
CHANGE YOUR WORLD!

ORDER TODAY

BOOK & MASTERCLASS

There are three kinds of people in the world. The wills, the won'ts, and the can'ts. The first accomplish everything. The second oppose everything. The third fail in everything. Countless Americans make their way home from work each day, stopping at their mailboxes to grab another fistful of bills, so they can go inside and figure out a way to keep things afloat for another thirty days. Whether you're stuck in that rut or doing everything you can to avoid it, best-selling author and success coach Dr. Dave Martin can help.

Embracing the principles in Mindset Matters Coaching Program will cause you to:

- Live an exceptional life.
- Do extraordinary things.
- Achieve your goals.
- Leave your mark on the world!

Follow Dr. Dave's formula for success, and you'll eventually find yourself doing the things that others only dream about doing and going places where others can only dream about going. A person with the right thinking becomes part of the solution for mankind, not part of the problem.

davemartin.org

AMERICA'S #1 CHRISTIAN SUCCESS COACH PRESENTS TO YOU
THE DAVE MARTIN PODCAST,
SUCCESS MADE SIMPLE!

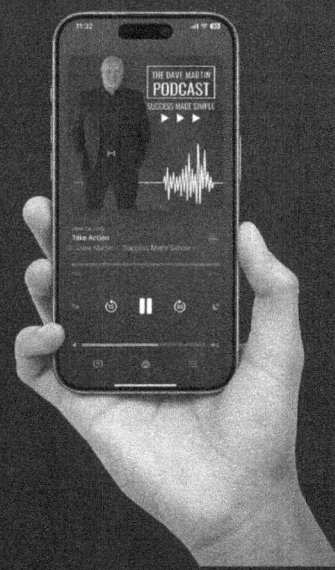

Dr. Dave Martin's "Success Made Simple" podcast is a dynamic platform that distills decades of expertise from a renowned success coach and motivator. Each episode offers actionable strategies for personal and professional growth, delivered with Dr. Martin's signature blend of enthusiasm and wisdom.

Named Top Ten Forbes Podcast, it engages listeners with practical advice on leadership, mindset mastery, and achieving peak performance. The podcast's clarity and relevance appeal to diverse audiences, providing invaluable tools to navigate challenges and maximize potential. Whether you're a seasoned entrepreneur or aspiring leader, "Success Made Simple" promises empowering content to propel you towards success.

Search Apple iTunes for The Dave Martin Podcast
or visit davemartin.org/podcast.